IMAGES OF WAR

M1 ABRAMS

IMAGES OF WAR

M1 ABRAMS

RARE PHOTOGRAPHS FROM WARTIME ARCHIVES

DAVID DOYLE

Pen & Sword
MILITARY
AN IMPRINT OF PEN & SWORD BOOKS LTD.
YORKSHIRE – PHILADELPHIA

First published in Great Britain in 2019 by
Pen & Sword Military
An imprint of
Pen & Sword Books Ltd
Yorkshire – Philadelphia

ISBN 978 1 52673 877 6

Typeset in 12/14.5 Gill Sans by
Aura Technology and Software Services, India
Printed and bound in Europe by Printworks Global Ltd

Pen & Sword Books Limited incorporates the imprints of Atlas, Archaeology, Aviation, Discovery, Family History, Fiction, History, Maritime, Military, Military Classics, Politics, Select, Transport, True Crime, Air World, Frontline Publishing, Leo Cooper, Remember When, Seaforth Publishing, The Praetorian Press, Wharncliffe Local History, Wharncliffe Transport, Wharncliffe True Crime and White Owl.

For a complete list of Pen & Sword titles please contact

PEN & SWORD BOOKS LIMITED
47 Church Street, Barnsley, South Yorkshire, S70 2AS, England
E-mail: enquiries@pen-and-sword.co.uk
Website: www.pen-and-sword.co.uk

or
PEN AND SWORD BOOKS
1950 Lawrence Rd, Havertown, PA 19083, USA
E-mail: Uspen-and-sword@casematepublishers.com
Website: www.penandswordbooks.com

Contents

Acknowledgements

None of these books would be possible without a great deal of help from my friends, some old, some new. This is particularly true in the case of this book, for which I leaned heavily on Rob Ervin; Don Moriarty; John Charvat, LTC(R); Russ Adams; Mike Mummey; Gary Owsley; Tom Kailbourn Scott Taylor and Scott Hamric, Third Armored Cavalry Regiment historian. My wonderful wife Denise also deserves thanks, especially for willingly helping with the photos for this book, despite the searing summer heat of Fort Hood, Texas and Fort Riley, Kansas.

All photos are by the author unless otherwise credited.

Introduction

As the Abrams closes in on forty years of service, it is inevitable that many books and thousands of pages have been written about the M1. This volume won't attempt to *tell* the story of evolution and service of this armored fighting vehicle; rather it is the intent of this volume to *show* you the evolution of the vehicle and provide you with a glimpse into the conditions under which America's fighting men took it into combat.

This book will present many of the detail changes of three major variants of the series, using photographs of existing examples of the vehicle. This volume presents an early prototype XM1, an M1E1, two M1A1s and an M1A2 SEP, not just of museum specimens but also active vehicles in use by US troops.

For those interested in a narrative of the development of the Abrams, we recommend the companion 'Images of War' book on the Abrams written by Michael Green. By design, there is very little duplication between this volume and Michael's.

The story of the Abrams begins in the late 1960s when the threat of Soviet armor developments forced the US to look for a suitable replacement for the M60 series. A joint venture between the US and West Germany to build a suitable common main battle tank brought about the unorthodox and terribly expensive MBT70. It never saw series production. When this program was cancelled in 1970, a quest for a more cost-effective tank was begun.

The constant development, upgrade and conversion of the series have kept the Abrams at the forefront of main battle tank technology, and it has proven itself on the battlefield time and time again. The Abrams is entering its fourth decade of service with US forces and the plan is to keep the vehicle in the United States' inventory through as late as 2040.

The original design of the M1 was conceived to allow the installation of the smoothbore M256 main gun with only minimal modification. The gun was a German Rheinmetall design for the Leopard II. With additional improvements to the armor, transmission, engine and the addition of an integrated nuclear, biological and chemical system, the new production M1A1 Abrams was standardized in 1984, with the first production vehicles delivered in 1985. Production at the Detroit Arsenal was now under the control of General Dynamics Land Systems. The production of the M1A1 ended in 1993 with more than 4,500 produced.

The new main gun greatly increased the tank's firepower. In 1988 a layer of depleted uranium (DU) was added to the special armor array in the front of the tank. This gave the tank unprecedented protection for the crew. The tanks were also equipped internally with powered blast doors that separated the turret crew from the ammunition storage in the turret's rear. This also increased crew survivability in case the tank was penetrated in this area.

The story of the M1A1 will be forever linked with images of the First Gulf War of 1991. Never in the 100-year history of armored warfare has such a dominant weapon appeared on the battlefield with almost complete impunity from its adversaries. In that brief conflict the tank achieved an almost perfect balance of firepower, mobility and protection.

This pair of Abrams from the US First Armored Division is conducting a combat patrol in Tal Afar, Iraq on 20 February 2006. Though a far cry from the environment for which the Abrams was envisioned, the Abrams has ably proven its effectiveness. (*US Air Force photo by Staff Sergeant Aaron Allmon*)

Above: The MBT70 incorporated a number of unorthodox components beyond the gun. The suspension would allow the vehicle to be raised and lowered overall, or at the front or rear. The entire crew operated in the turret, the driver having a rotating position in the left front. The gun was to feed with an automatic ammunition loading system, reducing the crew to three. When the MBT70 program was ended the army began development of a more cost-effective solution for a new tank. (*Patton Museum*)

Opposite above: By the late 1960s the M60 series was in need of replacement to keep pace with the threat of new Russian armor. The M60 was basically an evolutionary design that had begun with the M26 Pershing of 1945 with a wide variety of improvements to automotive systems, armor and firepower. This M60A1 is being put through its paces at the test track at the Detroit Tank Arsenal. (*Patton Museum*)

Opposite below: A joint effort between the US and West Germany in the late 1960s worked to develop a common main battle tank for both armies. The product of this venture was the MBT70. The extremely expensive and complicated design was equipped with a 152mm gun capable of firing both conventional rounds and a wire-guided anti-tank missile. The escalating costs of the design forced Congress to end the US involvement in the program in January 1970. The second US prototype is seen pictured here. (*Patton Museum*)

One of the Chrysler XMI pilot vehicles undergoes testing at Fort Knox, Kentucky. Following Chrysler winning the development contract in late 1976, extensive testing was done of the pilot vehicles at several military and private proving grounds. (*Patton Museum*)

Chapter 1

The XM1

The final outcome of almost a decade of development was the M1 Abrams. The new tank retained the 105mm gun of the M60A3 which it replaced. The development program had pitted designs from both General Motors and Chrysler against each other. Chrysler was eventually awarded the contract for its gas turbine-powered design. The layout of the tank was more conventional than the MBT70 design, with the exception of the turbine powertrain. The new tank was named Abrams in honor of the late General Creighton W. Abrams, former armor commander and Army Chief of Staff. (*Patton Museum*)

An early prototype XMI was displayed for many years at the Patton Museum of Armor at Fort Knox, Kentucky. The tank had undergone numerous tests at the base throughout the late 1970s. This tank is from a batch of three that were refurbished in 1979 with the latest features to be incorporated in the production vehicles. (*Don Moriarty*)

The hull sides are fitted with both Chobham armored 'ballistic' and plate steel unarmored 'non-ballistic' skirts. Left-side No. 1 & 2 skirts are ballistic, as are No. 1 through 4 on the right side. The No. 7 skirt seen here was modified on later production variants to allow mud to escape from the sprocket area. (*Don Moriarty*)

The turret and hull were made up from large rolled steel components that give the tank its signature angular appearance. The boxy shape made it possible to install a revolutionary armor array within the front surfaces. Called Chobham armor, the new system incorporated various layers of steel and ceramics to provide protection against the latest kinetic energy and chemical energy anti-tank weapons. (*Don Moriarty*)

The rear grille area is divided into three sections. The turbine exhaust is centered and flanked on each side by air outlets for the transmission oil coolers. These grilles help to reduce the thermal signature of the vehicle when seen from the front on the battlefield. (*Don Moriarty*)

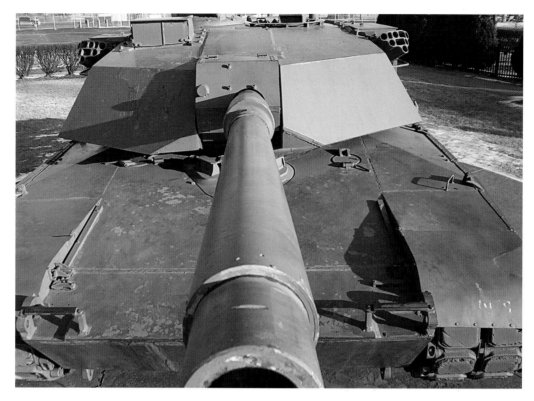

The XM1's main gun was the rifled M68 105mm with a thermal shroud, which was a derivative of the British L7. It was capable of firing all the common NATO ammunition. Fears that the 120mm gun then in development would not be available in time to field the new tank led to the use of the 105mm gun. The ability to mount the 120mm gun when available was a part of the original design philosophy. (*Don Moriarty*)

The forward portion of the turret was fitted with an armor package nearly 2ft thick, providing unprecedented protection for the crew. The gunner's primary sight is mounted in an armored box on the right front of the turret often referred to as the doghouse. The armored doors seen closed here protect the sight from light weapons' fire when not in use. (*Don Moriarty*)

The commander's weapon station (CWS) on the XM1 featured the early feed tray and ammunition box that was parallel to the M2 .50 Caliber MG. The CWS has five vision blocks and a multi position hatch that allows the hatch to be full closed, fully open and open protected which provides the commander the ability so see out through a narrow gap while having protection with the hatch over his head. (*Don Moriarty*)

The loader was provided with a hatch in the turret roof to the left of the commander's position. The hatch mounts a periscope that could be interchanged with the driver's thermal driving periscope. Around the loader's hatch is a skate rail for an M240 7.62mm machine gun. (*Don Moriarty*)

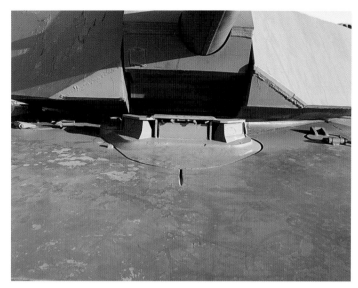

The driver's hatch is placed at the rear of the 2in-thick glacis plate. The glacis plate is sloped at 82 degrees from the vertical, providing excellent protection. The large hatch casting has three periscopes with an overlapping view of a 120-degree frontal arc. The driver's clear center periscope seen here can be interchanged with a passive night viewer. The notch in the hull top forward of the hatch is to drain water away from the hatch seal area. (*Don Moriarty*)

The driver is seated on the centerline of the lower hull in a semi-reclined position, although driving with the head above the hatch opening is not authorized when the turret is in operation. His seat can be raised into a position allowing him to operate the vehicle with his head out of the hatch. In the foreground to the left of the hatch is an armored door covering the forward fuel tank filler. (*Don Moriarty*)

The front fenders are capable of being folded up for servicing the vehicle or protecting them from damage while moving the vehicle in tight confines. The fender is held in place by a large latch on its inboard side. (*Don Moriarty*)

The contour of the hull construction and overhang of the turret cheeks are evident in this view. The turret design was conceived to utilize the largest possible ring diameter and mount the main gun as far forward as possible. (*Don Moriarty*)

The elevation of the main gun provides a good view of the details of the gun shield. A 7.62mm coaxial mount machine gun was mounted in the aperture to the right of the main gun. The opening has been blanked off on this display tank. (*Don Moriarty*)

The right side of the turret mounts an open stowage basket, a stowage box and a smoke grenade-launcher. Each launcher carried six grenades to provide smoke cover for the vehicle and could be fired from within the tank. The smoke grenades cover a 120-degree arc at about 30 yards from the vehicle. (*Don Moriarty*)

The electrical power conduit for the launcher is protected by a cover. It exits the turret through the roof rather than compromise the armor of the turret sides. The storage box is hinged to open to the outside away from the tank. (*Don Moriarty*)

The M250 launchers are large cast parts and have cast-in foundry marks on their tops. They are attached to the turret by a sheet metal bracket fixed by bolts welded to the turret side armor plate. The M250 units are patterned after a British design. (*Don Moriarty*)

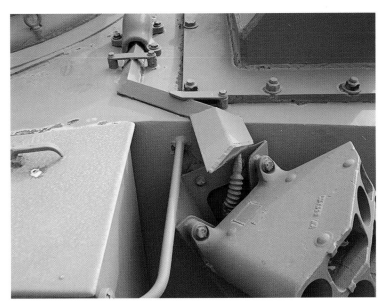

The left side of the turret was also equipped with a stowage box and open stowage rack. The vehicle's tow cable was stored in clips along the side of the turret below the box. The rectangular opening in the hull side above the armored skirts houses the external firing handles for the engine-compartment fire suppression system. (*Don Moriarty*)

The grille in the forward left engine deck is the sponson pre-cleaner and the combustion air intake for the AGT-1500 turbine engine. The air is filtered two more times by another pre-cleaner and three air filters called 'Vee Packs'. Although the Abrams series can burn multiple fuels and initially used Diesel, US forces currently use either JP-5 or JP-8. (*Don Moriarty*)

The engine deck of the XM1 is rather simple when compared to later tanks. It lacks some access panels in the rear deck plate. The XM1 and production M1s were not equipped with the prominent rear turret stowage rack. (*Don Moriarty*)

The simple, flat rolled armor panel over the engine compartment of the XM-1 was very different from the complicated array of cast armored louvers found on its predecessor, the M60 series. (*Don Moriarty*)

The turret rear has two rows of tie-down points or footman loops for securing gear with web straps. The fixture on the left corner of the turret rear is the mount for the receiver/transmitter antenna. The XM1 was equipped with the AN/VRC-12 radio system. (*Don Moriarty*)

The XM1's main ammunition storage is in the rear of the turret. It is separated from the crew compartment by large sliding blast doors. The three blow-out panels in the roof of the turret are designed to vent the energy of any ammunition explosion if the turret is penetrated by an anti-tank round. In the foreground is the folded mast for the fire-control system's wind sensor. (*Don Moriarty*)

The blow-out panels are seen here from the turret's left side. The fixture between the panels and the loader's hatch is a cover for the electrical conduit that supplies power to the left-side smoke grenade-launcher. (*Don Moriarty*)

On the right rear corner is a mount for an additional antenna with a removable cover. The turret side stowage basket was constructed of steel rods welded to support brackets. The XM1 was approved for limited production in May 1979. (*Don Moriarty*)

Chapter 2

The Improved
Performance M1

Above: As production of the M1 Abrams ramped up in the early 1980s, General Dynamics undertook a program to upgrade the M1 tank. This vehicle, the Improved Product M1 (IPM1), incorporated a range of revisions intended to improve its performance and protection as well as to better adapt the Abrams to the planned transition from the 105mm gun M68A1 to the 120mm gun XM256. Improvements were made to the transmission, final drives, suspension, main gun mount and armor. An IPM1 is seen here undergoing tests at Aberdeen Proving Ground. (*Patton Museum*)

Opposite above: The test vehicle IPM1 at Aberdeen, like all other IPM1s, was armed with the 105mm gun M68A1. This vehicle had the mount and cradle for a .50-caliber machine gun at the commander's cupola, but the gun was not installed. An amber caution light was mounted over the turret roof. The exterior of the IPM1 was virtually indistinguishable from a stock M1 Abrams. (*Patton Museum*)

Part of the IPM1 improvements was a detachable stowage rack for placement on the rear of the turret bustle. The rack is not present in this photo, but the mounting brackets or lugs for the rack are in view. There is one on each side of the top of the bustle (one is slightly inboard of the left radio antenna), and there are two mounting brackets on the lower plate of the bustle, two of which are visible. (*Patton Museum*)

Above: In a view of the right side of the IPM1 tested at Aberdeen Proving Ground, protruding from the gun shield next to the 105mm gun barrel is the extension tube for the 7.62mm M240 coaxial machine gun. The tube functioned as a flash suppressor to reduce the visual signature of the machine gun when firing at night. (*Patton Museum*)

Opposite above: In a rear view of an IPM1, all five mounting brackets for the turret-bustle stowage rack are visible: one on each upper corner of the bustle and three on the lower rear plate of the bustle. At the center of the upper rear plate of the bustle is the wind sensor, to the right of which is the storage bracket for the sensor. (*Patton Museum*)

Opposite below: The IPM1 had an improved final drive featuring a planetary gear, with a gear ratio of 4.667:1 as opposed to the 4.30:1 ratio of the M1 Abrams tank. Like the M1, the IPM1's drive sprockets had eleven teeth and a retaining ring. (*Patton Museum*)

The commander's weapon station (CWS) on the turret roof of the IPM1 was the same as that on the M1 Abrams tank, with a periscope and a forward-tilted pedestal for the .50-caliber machine gun. To the front of the CWS is the 'doghouse', or gunner's primary sight (GPS) housing, with its left door open. (*Patton Museum*)

Details of an IPM1 with its turret traversed to the rear are seen from above. To the left, part of the turret-bustle stowage rack is visible. Also in view are the CWS, the loader's hatch, the GPS housing and the top of the shield for the 105mm gun. A total of 894 IPM1 tanks were produced, with deliveries running from October 1984 until production closed in May 1986. (*Patton Museum*)

Chapter 3

The M1E1

On display at Fort Hood, Texas is one of the fourteen prototype 120mm Gun Tank M1E1s. It was basically an M1 Abrams Main Battle Tank with a 120mm Gun XM256 replacing the 105mm Gun M68E1. The M1E1 also incorporated new ammunition-stowage equipment, a modified fire-control system, improved armor protection and a nuclear, biological and chemical (NBC) crew-protection and cooling system. The NBC system is an overpressure system that caused the interior of the tank to have a higher air pressure than the surrounding atmosphere to keep chemical agents out of the tank.

On the middle of the 120mm gun barrel is a bore evacuator, significantly larger and more rounded than the bore evacuator of the M1 Abrams 105mm gun. The bore evacuator acted to extract fumes from the barrel after the gun was fired. (*John Charvat*)

The gunshield of the M1E1, where the 120mm gun barrel enters the front of the turret, was identical to that of the M1 Abrams. Below the gunshield is the driver's hatch cover with three periscopes for viewing to the front and to the sides. (*John Charvat*)

From the side, the Fort Hood MIEI looks virtually the same as an MI Abrams Main Battle Tank, with the exception of the 120mm gun and its distinctive bore evacuator. The MIEI used a shorter MI turret, not the longer one found on production MIAIs and IPMIs. Not visible is the MIEI's significantly upgraded final drive and transmission.

Housed inside the slightly raised structure on the sponson at the center of the photo, between the stowage box on the side of the turret and the top of the track skirts, is the integrated NBC protection and environmental control system. (*John Charvat*)

Details of the front of the right side of the MIEI turret and the side skirts are portrayed. Hinges and locking pins for the side skirts are in view. On the side of the turret at the center are a tow-cable holder and, to the front of it, a splash shield. (*John Charvat*)

The housing for the NBC system would undergo further revisions on other MIEIs, including the addition of a hooded port forward of the rectangular opening for the external fire-extinguisher actuating handle, to the right in this photo. (*John Charvat*)

The rear panel of the side skirts is of the original design as used on the M1 Abrams. Some M1E1s had a modified rear skirt panel with a large cut-out at the lower rear, intended to prevent the build-up of mud around the drive sprocket. (*John Charvat*)

To make the tank less susceptible to thermal targeting, grilles at the rear of the hull diffuse engine exhaust across the breadth of the tank's rear. The stowage rack on the rear of the turret bustle was an addition not originally present on the M1. (*John Charvat*)

36

Above: The M1E1 at Fort Hood is viewed from the right side. The tank's 120mm Gun XM256 has a bore of 208.7in, about 2in shorter than that of the M1 Abrams' 105mm Gun M68A1. Total weight of the gun and mount was 4,200lb.

Opposite above: Lifting eyes protrude from each side of the top of the exhaust grille. On each side of the rear of the hull below the grille is a tow eye, and between them is a towing pintle. Small eyes are welded to the upper rear of the hull above the exhaust grille.

Opposite below: On the right side of the M1E1 turret are stowage racks, stowage bin and, along the bottom edge, tow-cable holders. Atop the turret are the gunner's primary-sight ballistic shield cover and the commander's .50-caliber machine-gun mount.

On the right side of the gunshield of the M1E1 is the extension tube for the 7.62mm M240 coaxial ('coax') machine gun, which served as a flash suppressor. To the top left is the front of the gunner's primary-sight ballistic shield cover. (*John Charvat*)

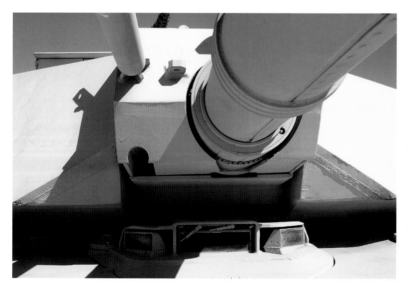

On the lower right front of the gunshield of the M1E1 is a round opening for the gunner's auxiliary sight, used when his main sight was not operating. Also visible are the thermal jacket on the 120mm gun and the wipers for the center periscope. (*John Charvat*)

Some MIEI prototypes had armor plates welded to the frontal plates of the turret to each side of the main gun to simulate the extra armor that was projected for the next model of the Abrams MBT, but this MIEI lacked that extra armor plating.

The driver's hatch cover operated by lifting up slightly and pivoting to the right. When buttoned up in the tank, the driver used these three fixed periscopes to see outside. The center periscope has two small wipers, mounted above the glass.

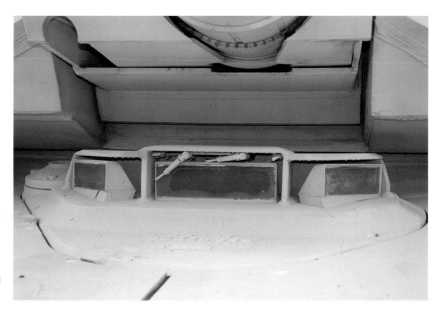

The inner side of the left suspension is observed from under the front of the hull. Each of the seven dual road wheels was mounted on a high-strength torsion bar. The wheels were mounted with size 25-5.69 tires. Tracks were the model T156.

In a view of the right headlight, the brush guard consists of a metal bar fastened with hex screws to a raised lug on one side and to the top of the lift ring on the other. The hinged fender (left) is held down by a torsion-spring latch.

Each headlight assembly consists of a service headlight towards the vehicle's right side of the housing and a blackout marker lamp with a rectangular slot on the front on the left side of the housing. Aft of the headlight, under the turret, is one of four fuel filler caps.

The left front corner of the M1E1 at Fort Hood is viewed from above, with the left fender to the right and the front of the hull to the bottom. The rear of the headlight housing is bolted to a headlight bracket, which in turn is bolted to the glacis. On the inboard side and to the rear of the fender is the L-shaped fender latch. (*John Charvat*)

In a view over the front right of the turret of the MIEI, to the right are the cover for the gunner's primary sight and, to the rear of it, the commander's weapon station (CWS). To the left is a stowage locker with two latch handles mounted on the lid.

The .50-caliber MG HB on the CWS was fired remotely using a sight and hand controls inside the cupola. The entire CWS could be rotated and periscopes were mounted on it to provide the commander with vision while inside the tank.

To the side of the CWS is the loader's hatch, the cover of which was equipped with a rotating periscope. A C-shaped skate mount partially surrounding the hatch provided a mount for a 7.62mm M240 machine gun, which was hand-operated.

The loader's hatch is observed. To the right is the M240 machine-gun mount, equipped with hand grips, cradle and holder for an ammunition box. Atop the turret bustle are two blow-off covers over the 120mm ammunition lockers. (*John Charvat*)

Chapter 4

The M1A1

An early-production M1A1 is seen on display at Fort Knox, Kentucky. The M256 120mm smooth-bore main gun was a development of the German Rheinmetall weapon and replaced the 105mm M68 in the M1A1. The gun tube is equipped with a thermal shroud and bore evacuator.

Above: The left side of the hull is laid out in much the same manner as the right. The headlight has a slit for a blackout light on its outboard side. A spare track end connector is stowed on the fender latch. (*Don Moriarty*)

Opposite above: This late-production M1A1 was photographed while in active service. The late-production tanks have a blanked-off aperture in the left-side turret roof to allow installation later of the commander's independent thermal viewer. This device was eliminated from the early designs as a cost-saving measure. (*Don Moriarty*)

Opposite below: The right front portion of the hull is equipped with a headlight and a heavy brush guard. The front fender has a thick rubber skirt attached to its forward edge. A common sight on the Abrams is the addition by the crew of a track end connector to the fender latch. This added more weight to prevent it from rattling while driving. (*Don Moriarty*)

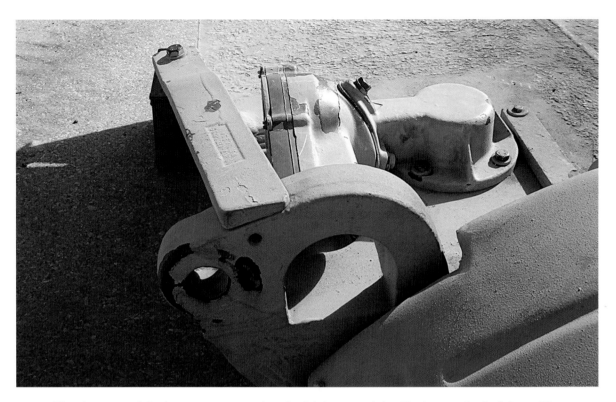

The sheet metal fenders are contoured to fit tightly around the lift ring on the hull front. The headlight mounting is very robust. Earlier US tank designs had headlight fittings that were much more susceptible to damage. (*Don Moriarty*)

The headlight brush guard is attached to the front hull lift ring. Apparent is the texture of the non-skid surface applied to the glacis armor. Identification numbers made with weld beads are on the forward edge of the glacis. (*Don Moriarty*)

Above: On the inner side of the right front fender is a clip for the torsion spring-style latch. This device would allow the fender to spring back without damage if struck, while holding it securely in the forward position. Weld bead numbers are visible on the glacis edge.

Below: The left-side fender has the same latch arrangement as does the right fender. When the spring latch is released from the clip as here, the fender can be easily lifted for servicing.

Above: The front portion of the lower hull mounts a tow lug on each side. The lugs mount quick-release towing hooks. A cable is slipped over the end of the hook, and then turned 90 degrees to secure it. (*Don Moriarty*)

Below: The left-side tow lug also mounts a hook. The hooks are held in place with a large pin secured by quick-release cotter pins. The track end connectors, 'wedge nuts' and bolts are visible behind the tow lug. (*Don Moriarty*)

Above: The driver's hatch cover is a large casting that houses three periscopes. The center periscope is equipped with two short windshield wipers as well as night vision and a thermal viewer on the M1A1. The latter fittings were a part of the improvement program of the M1. A clear vision block can be substituted with either a passive or thermal viewer. A bullet splash lip was added to the hatch as a result of small-arms incidents in Operation DESERT STORM. (*Don Moriarty*)

At the top of the glacis plate on the right is the filler for the front fuel tank with an armored cover. The driver's hatch opens back to the right into this area and is secured by clips to prevent closing while driving. (*Don Moriarty*)

The driver's hatch is held in place by a safety catch at the rear of the hatch and a handle on the gearbox inside the driver's compartment. A safety catch at the rear of the hatch holds it open. The wipers are manually operated; the sheet metal cover behind the center periscope protects the washer fluid hose. (*Don Moriarty*)

Above: Various colors are visible on the surface of optical devices on modern tanks due to coatings that shield the crew from battlefield lasers. High-powered laser devices used for range-finding and target designation can be very damaging to the human eye. (*Don Moriarty*)

Below: This worm's eye view gives a good indication of the low silhouette and extreme slope of the armor of the Abrams. These features were key to maximizing the survivability of the M1A1's crew on the modern battlefield.

The track skirts and their hinging system are visible from the left front quarter. The massive length of the turret was necessary to house the armor array, ammunition stowage at the rear and provide adequate room for the crew. (*Don Moriarty*)

The T158 track is equipped with a separate removable rubber pad and was first installed on the M1A1. It replaced the T156 track with an integral pad to save cost. The T156s were only providing 700 to 800 miles of use before needing replacement. (*Don Moriarty*)

The forward plate of the armored side skirts is held by a latch to a post mounted to the hull side behind the compensating idler wheel. At the bottom of the skirt is a loop of cable for a crew step. (*Don Moriarty*)

All tanks, no matter how advanced, require considerable hands-on maintenance. The hinged armored side skirts provide access to the suspension, an area that requires considerable preventative maintenance. Grease fittings and wheel bearings must be properly lubricated after operating the vehicle. (*Don Moriarty*)

The NBC system that was introduced on the M1A1 was installed in the area formerly occupied by a shallow stowage bin in the left hull side. The projection on the bottom of the turret bustle is a protection for the NBC back-up system inlet. (*Don Moriarty*)

The thick armored plates that attach the NBC system are bolted to the left hull side. The top edge of the armored skirt has a thin flexible seal that is held against the hull side. (*Don Moriarty*)

Just aft of the NBC system is the external control handle for the engine-compartment fire-suppression equipment. It can be fired by the exiting crew or by nearby troops. The Halon system has infrared sensors in the interior and engine bay to automatically operate in the event of fire. (*Don Moriarty*)

The suspension swing arms are mounted to the hull side by large cast plates that also serve to anchor the opposite side torsion bar. (*Don Moriarty*)

The center guide horn of the track makes contact with the inner portion of the road wheels, giving them the shiny worn appearance. (*Don Moriarty*)

The drive sprocket on the M1A1 is an eleven-tooth design. The problem of the early M1 tanks throwing tracks was alleviated by various measures, including altering the shape of the last skirt and adding holes to the outer portion of the hub for mud to exit. Proper driver training and increasing track tension also helped to solve the problem. (*Don Moriarty*)

The left rear hull corner of the M1A1 armor protects the rear fuel tank. The fuel filler securing chain hangs down the side of the tank. The flexible seal between the hull and skirt is secured by bolts and a metal strip to the top of the skirt.

In order to allow the right and left transmission oil-cooler grilles to swing away from the rear hull, the hinges must be quite deep. With the three grilles swung away, great access to the transmission is provided.

The center section of the grille is discolored by the heat of the engine exhaust. A tow pintle is mounted on the lower hull rear plate just below the center grille. Two tow lugs are outboard on the plate. (*Don Moriarty*)

The exhaust grille vanes are protected from damage by a guard made up of welded bar stock and rods. They are attached to the vanes by clips and bolts. (*Don Moriarty*)

Marine mechanics work on an engine that has been removed from an M1A1 tank of Company A, 2nd Tank Battalion at Camp Habbaniyah, Iraq on 29 June 2006. On the front end of the engine, to the lower left, is the low-pressure compressor. On top of the engine to the far right is the exhaust duct. (*USMC*)

Above: Mechanics maneuver a power pack into the engine compartment of an Abrams tank, USMC registration number 572393, at Camp Coyote, Kuwait during the war in Afghanistan. The construction of the power pack made it relatively easy to remove the transmission, engine and coolers as a unit, using a 5-ton wrecker or crane. (*USMC*)

Opposite above: The compact size of the Avco Lycoming AGT-1500 gas turbine engine is apparent when displayed outside the tank. In this rear view, the radiator-like assemblies to either side of this rear view are oil coolers for the X1100 transmission.

Opposite below: The AGT-1500 viewed from the left side, with the intake on the left of the picture and the gray sheet metal exhaust duct above. The engine provides 1,500 horsepower and makes the tank capable of amazing performance for such a heavy machine.

Above: Initial development of the gas turbine engine was slowed by concerns about costs. However, after complete development and series production, the AGT-1500 costs and longevity came into line with alternative Diesel powertrains.

Opposite above: At the front of the engine is the large air intake. The Abrams' engine is not very fuel-efficient but provides a great amount of power and is very easy to remove and replace in the field.

Opposite below: The outboard transmission cooler grilles are similar in construction to the exhaust grille with the exception of the hinges. It is evident that the heat from the oil coolers is not as great as that of the engine exhaust. (*Don Moriarty*)

Above: The rear fender skirts are missing from this Abrams, exposing green CARC paint around its mounting are and exposing the return of the T-158 track. The skirts were often removed to prevent build up of mud. An example of the rear skirt can be seen on page 35. (*Don Moriarty*)

Opposite above: On both sides of the lower hull rear plate are small access panels (here removed) that cover the drains for the transmission final drives. The desert camo paint has been scuffed down to the original NATO verdant camouflage colors. (*Don Moriarty*)

Opposite below: The right-side access plate, which covers a drain from the transmission final drive, has been removed in this view. The chipped paint gives some idea of the thickness of the coating applied to these vehicles. The paint has flaked in rather large areas due to abrasion. (*Don Moriarty*)

The taillight assemblies are a common part to most US-built military vehicles. They mount a large red plastic lens with a slit for the blackout light in the lower portion of the housing.

Just inboard of the right-side taillight are mounted the slave receptacle and an infantry phone box. (*Don Moriarty*)

The lower box contains an infantry telephone. This allows troops in close contact with the tank to communicate to the commander. (*Don Moriarty*)

The top box contains the slave receptacle. In the event of low batteries on a vehicle, a heavy jumper cable, known as a slave cable, can be plugged into this receptacle and that of a second vehicle, joining their electrical systems. (*Don Moriarty*)

Above: The power attachments for the slave receptacle exit the hull armor through an opening behind the taillight housing. (*Don Moriarty*)

Opposite above: The right rear fuel tank filler cover is secured by a locking pin. The pin is secured by a clip and has a chain to prevent it from being lost. When the pin is removed the armored cap flips forward to expose the fuel filler below. (*Don Moriarty*)

Opposite below: The battery box door and, to its left, screens for the engine oil cooler are visible on the right side of the tank. Inboard of the fuel tank covers is a plate covering the air cleaners. A large portion of the engine deck is set aside for filtering the huge amounts of intake air necessary for the operation of the turbine engine and cooling the transmission and engine oil. (*Don Moriarty*)

Above: The engine oil cooler screens on the right side of the engine deck bolt down to seal their edge against debris entering the engine compartment. Many failures of the early AGT- 1500 engines were due to dust ingestion. (*Don Moriarty*)

Opposite above: Here the left-side fuel filler's armored cover is seen from the rear. The locking pin is secured by a length of chain to a loop on the cover itself. (*Don Moriarty*)

Opposite below: The fuel filler at the left rear is provided with an armored cover. The JP-8 marking on the lid marks the type of fuel used in the tank. The US Army operates all Abrams on JP-8 jet fuel rather than JP-5 jet fuel. (*Don Moriarty*)

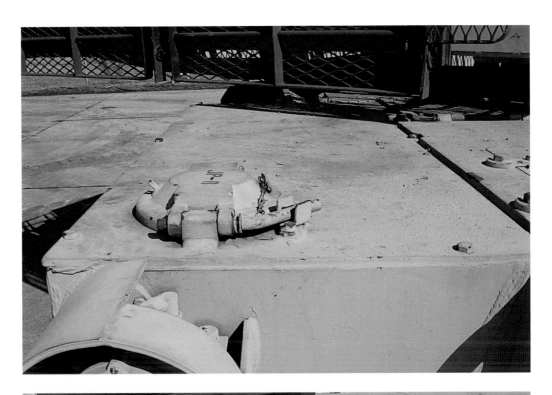

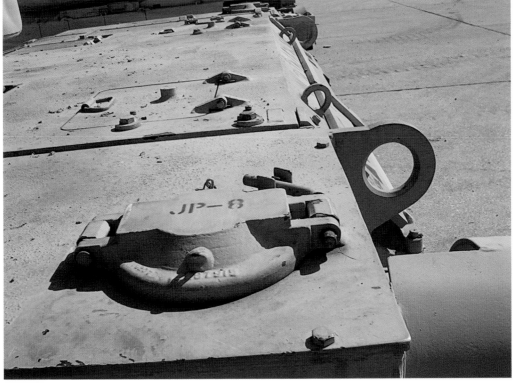

Above: The forward portion of the engine deck slopes downward, allowing the turret to be mounted to the hull at a much lower plane, thereby reducing the tank's silhouette. The deck is coated with anti-skid texture. The flush-mounted handles of the NBC system cover are in the foreground. (*Don Moriarty*)

Opposite above: Forward of the right hull top stowage box is the outlet for the right-side hull bilge pump. The bilge pump works just like that of a boat to remove water that may enter the tank and pool in the lower portions of the hull. (*Don Moriarty*)

Opposite below: This M1A1 Abrams exhibits signs of hard use. The paint on the hull and skirts is heavily chipped and abraded. The fleet of M1A1 vehicles has been constantly rebuilt at a facility at the Anniston Army Depot since the late 1990s. This practice of rebuilding has proved to be cheaper than building new vehicles. (*Don Moriarty*)

Above: M1A1s and the IPM1 were the first tanks to receive the removable rear turret bustle storage rack. Many tanks are seen with an auxiliary power unit attached in the left portion of the bustle rack. (*Don Moriarty*)

Opposite above: The bustle rack has been augmented by an additional extension on its rear. This was a very common feature on tanks used in the 2003 Gulf campaign. (*Don Moriarty*)

Opposite below: The bustle rack extension is of similar construction to the original rack, featuring a floor made of expanded metal. The extension is bolted to the larger original rack with brackets that attach to the uprights. (*Don Moriarty*)

Above: The bustle rack extension is capable of quickly being folded flat against the rear stowage rack when not in use. (*Don Moriarty*)

Opposite above: Here another Abrams is fitted with a bustle rack extension painted in European NATO colors. It is folded flat into the stowed position. (*Don Moriarty*)

Opposite below: From the rear the expanded metal screening in the bottom of the bustle rack extension is visible. Locking pins quickly secure the rack in its folded position or alternatively hold the extension side panels in place when the extension is in use. (*Don Moriarty*)

The rear turret bustle stowage rack is a removable design. It is held in place by four brackets with quick-release pins. The lower brackets are visible from below, with the clip for the release pins visible on the far side mount. (*Don Moriarty*)

Numerous details of a tank in service are visible in this right-side view. The road wheel tires are marked with spots of Desert Sand paint. The staining on the bore evacuator is probably from the cleaning solvent used to clean the inside of the bore evacuator after firing. (*Don Moriarty*)

Canvas covers are in place on the smoke grenade-launchers on the turret side. The clips for securing the cable are bright from wear and stained with oil. More numbers from weld beads are present on the edge of the turret armor. (*Don Moriarty*)

The right-side forward skirt panel has the paint badly worn around its securing latch. The fresh scratches that do not go all the way through the paint reveal the much brighter color of the unstained paint below. (*Don Moriarty*)

Above: More evidence of hard use on this tank; the crew has scuffed the paint on the turret face entering and exiting the vehicle. The base of the flash suppressor for the coaxial machine gun shows scorching and soot from firing the weapon. (*Don Moriarty*)

Opposite above: The lid of the right-side hull stowage bin is embossed with an 'X'-shaped pattern. Stamping the panel in this fashion strengthens the otherwise flimsy last panel. The lid is covered, as are most of the upper surfaces, with a non-skid coating. (*Don Moriarty*)

Opposite below: The rectangular storage box for smoke grenades is mounted just forward of the M250 launcher on the turret sides. The box holds six smoke rounds. (*Don Moriarty*)

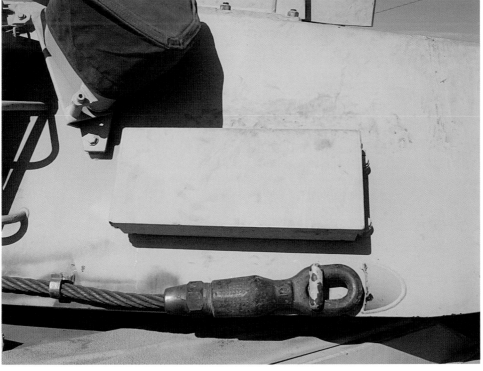

Above: MIAIs were fitted with a tubular flash suppressor for the coaxial mounted M240 7.62mm machine gun. This weapon is belt-fed and fired electronically by the gunner or commander. Spent rounds are caught in a tray below the gun. (*Don Moriarty*)

Opposite above: Photographed in Potts Motor Pool at Fort Knox, Kentucky on 29 July 2009, this MIAI was being used as a 'Boresight the MIAI' instructional vehicle for Marine Corps Tanker 'Trainees'. The USMC detachment attached with the US Army Armor Center regularly trains its future generations of Marine Corps tankers on Army tanks. (*Don Moriarty*)

Opposite below: The armored doors on the gunner's primary sight are open on this tank. The thermal imaging sight within this device is the heart of the fire-control system. The Abrams has unprecedented first-shot hit capabilities. (*Don Moriarty*)

Above: The M256 120mm gun is a smooth-bore weapon. This allows for extremely high velocity of modern kinetic energy rounds. The penetrators of these rounds are fin-stabilized. (*Don Moriarty*)

Opposite above: The M256 120mm gun mounts a rounded contour plastic bore evacuator. Pressure within the gun tube behind the exiting round is reduced as the gas leaks off through small holes in the tube within the extractor. (*Don Moriarty*)

Opposite below: The bore evacuator creates a slight lower-pressure situation between the breech and the evacuator so that when the breech opens, air flows into the tube, reducing the risk of flashback; extremely important in the Abrams due to the combustible cartridge cases of its ammunition. (*Don Moriarty*)

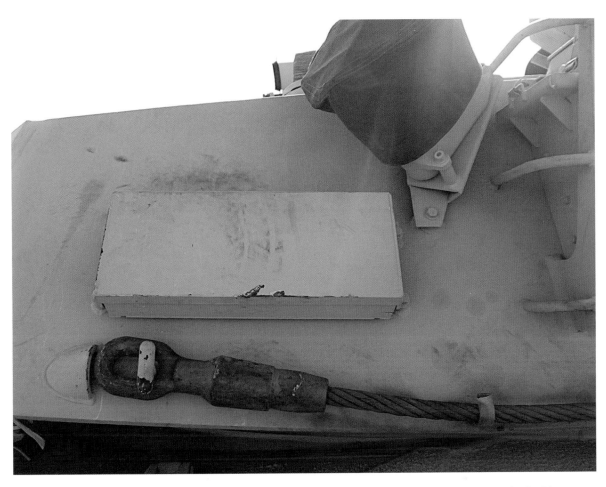

Above: Boot prints are visible on the smoke grenade storage box. The box is badly scratched with the paint chipped down to bare metal. (*Don Moriarty*)

Opposite above: The fire-control system monitors a number of variables to provide optimum ability to hit a target, such as wind speed, target movement and type of ammunition loaded. The end of the gun is equipped with a muzzle reference sensor that can read any bend in the barrel due to uneven heating of its surface. The gun is also equipped with an aluminum cover or thermal shroud to minimize this heating. (*Don Moriarty*)

Opposite below: For the fire-control system to function properly the gun barrel must be properly calibrated to the gunner's primary sight. This is achieved with this bore sighting device. The gun tube and gunner's sight are aligned to a fixed point at a specific distance with the gun at zero degrees elevation. (*Don Moriarty*)

Above: The panels stand proud of the roof plate. They are firmly attached to the turret and still provide armored protection from above. All but six of the forty rounds of the tank's main gun ammunition are stored in the turret bustle.

Right: Heavy weld beads join the cylindrical antenna mount at the right rear of the M1A1 turret. The Abrams has a number of systems to keep the crew in communication on the battlefield.

Opposite above: The M250 smoke grenade-launcher is mounted to the turret side armor on posts that attach to a mounting bracket. The same type of post-mounting arrangement is used for the stowage bin as well. (Don Moriarty)

Opposite below: The rear roof of the turret on the M1A1 is dominated by the two large blow-out panels above the ammunition storage. In the event of a penetration igniting the ammunition they allow a path for the energy to escape. (Don Moriarty)

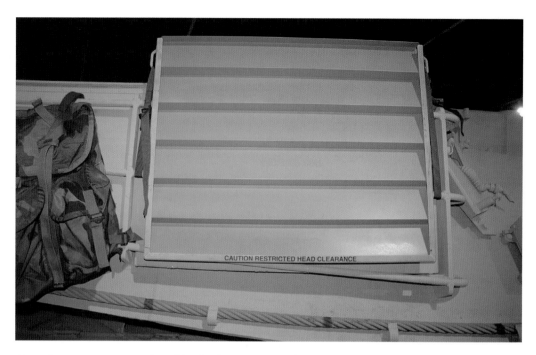

Above: In an attempt to reduce friendly-fire casualties, Coalition forces installed identification panels on their vehicles in front-line service. These louvered plastic panels were very distinctive when viewed through thermal sights.

Below: The turret rear stowage bins were introduced on the M1E1 and concurrently on IPM1 production. The bin is constructed of steel rod and sheet steel brackets with rounded corners.

The lower side of the bin is attached to the turret with a hinged-type mounting. The construction of the bin is significantly heavier than earlier US tank designs.

The floor of the stowage basket is formed from heavy-gauge steel screen. The use of screen provides the necessary strength, will keep small items secure and yet allow rainwater to drain out and dust to settle through rather than collecting.

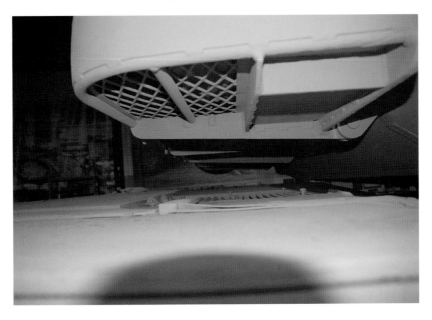

Above: The coaxially-mounted 7.62mm M240 machine gun is equipped with a large tubular flash suppressor on the Abrams. The weapon was a US-built version of the Belgian-designed FN MAG.

Opposite above: Mounting lugs for the Tellfare/Brewster Device surround the gun tube. Both were conceived as gunnery training devices. The Tellfare, which was used on a full-sized tank range, was a bolt-on mount for the M2 .50-caliber to allow it to be single-shot fired to save on ammunition cost. The Brewster device used an M16 and typically used a scaled range to fire at molded foam miniature tank models.

Opposite below: Above the gun shield is a rotor shield that serves to keep water and debris out of this area. The hinge arrangement allows the cover to move with the elevation of the main gun. The cover is constructed of a light-gauge metal. The welds that parallel the turret face denote the thickness of the massive array of armor laminated below.

Above: From above, the various panels that make up the turret roof are evident from the weld seams where they join.

Opposite above: The welds on the underside of the turret cheeks give some idea of the thickness of the outer layer of rolled armor plate in the massive armor array.

Opposite below: Details for the construction of the armored cover for the gunner's primary sight have changed from the XM1. Initially, the tanks used this type cover for the primary sight, but later versions did away with the angled rear, becoming square and featuring additional armor on the sides. The most important part of the Abrams' targeting system is its thermal sight. It is capable of reading slight differences in temperature between a target and its surroundings through rain, smoke, fog, camouflage nets and in the dark.

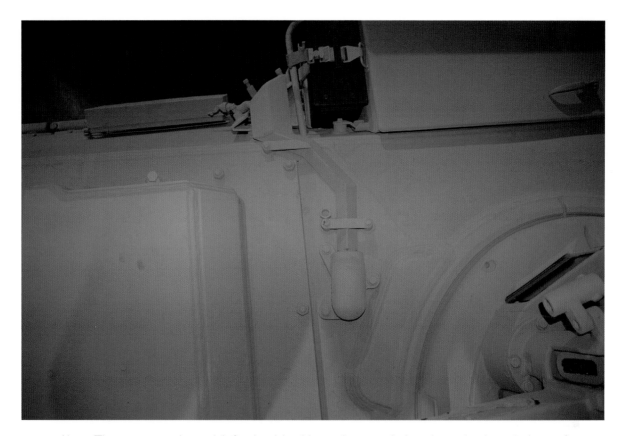

Above: The power supply conduit for the right-side smoke grenade-launcher exits through the roof forward of the commander's cupola. The launcher is missing on this example. The rectangular box forward of the launcher bracket is for carrying additional smoke grenades.

Opposite above: The Abrams is equipped with a commander's weapon station (CWS) mounting a variant of the Browning M2 .50-caliber heavy-barrel machine gun. There are back-up iron sights on the bottom of the mount. The TC looks through the Forward Unity Periscope (FUP) to use them. The sight for the M85 CWS .50-caliber machine-gun mount is below the weapon itself. The commander sights the weapon through his forward periscope. The cupola is fitted with six periscopes with laser shielding.

Opposite below: The commander's weapon station allowed the commander to operate from three different hatch positions: closed, open protected and open. The open position provided overhead protection, allowed for a full 360-degree view and provided back protection from the hatch plate.

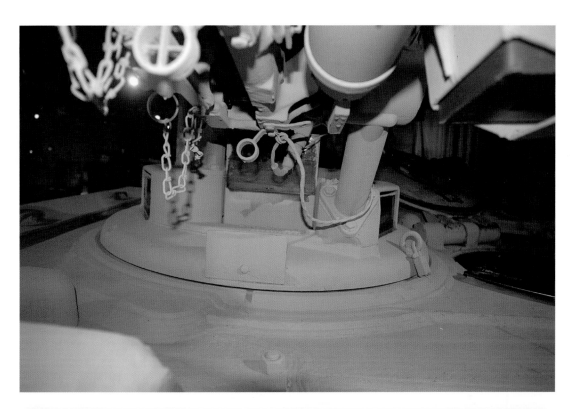

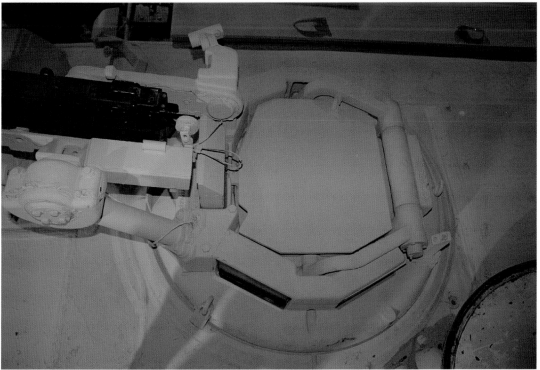

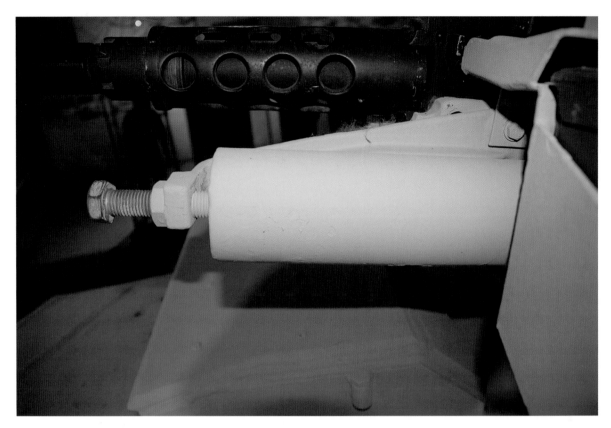

Above: The CWS mount was equipped with an M2 heavy-barrel Browning machine gun. The M2 is a formidable weapon for use against lightly-armored targets, aircraft and buildings. The gun could be fired remotely from within the turret but one had to leave the protection of the turret to reload the weapon.

Opposite above: The gun could be elevated on this pivot point on the left side of the mount. Crews learned that the gun could be traversed towards the loader's hatch and could be reloaded from that hatch with minimal exposure. The ammunition was stored in a standard box.

Opposite below: The loader's hatch, seen here open, is identical to the one on the XM1. The hatch was equipped with a 10in-wide periscope that rotated through 360 degrees. This periscope could be substituted for the driver's thermal/night vision periscope.

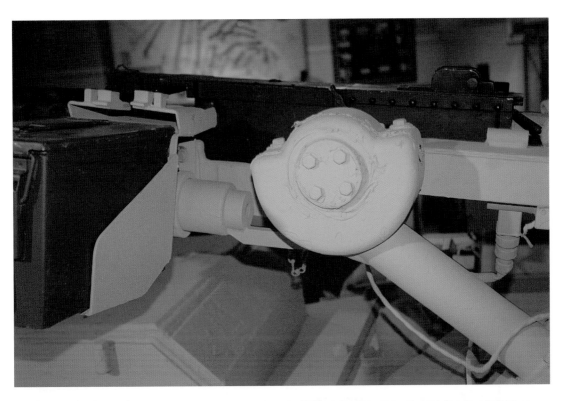

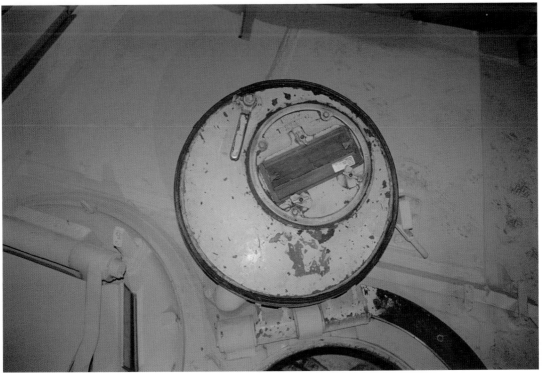

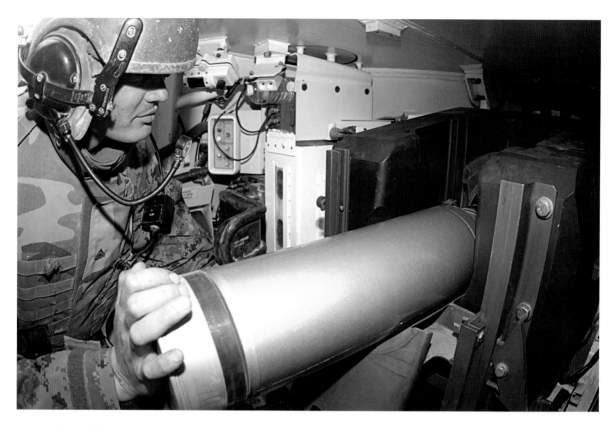

Above: The loader of a US Marine Corps MIAI Abrams tank shoves a 120mm round into the breech of the main gun during a live-firing exercise in An Najaf Province, Iraq on 24 January 2005. Most of the casing of the 120mm round is combustible, so that when the gun is fired only the metal base of the casing is ejected. (*USMC*)

Opposite above: The gutted interior of this display tank is missing all of its electronic gear. This affords an excellent view of the massive breach block of the M256 120mm gun. The recoil travel of the gun was 13 inches.

Opposite below: The left turret side is also equipped with a smoke grenade-launcher (missing here) and a box for additional grenades. A 200-round 7.62mm ammo box for the M240 is strapped in the location where a 100-round can of .50 caliber ammunition for the M2 is normally stowed.

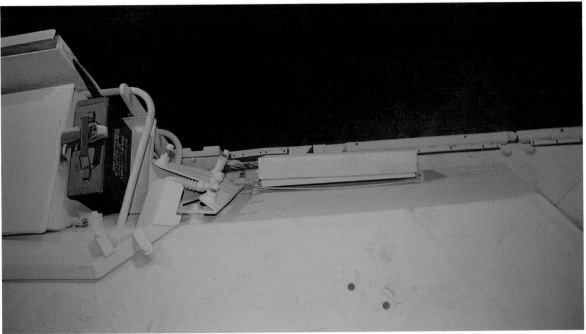

Above: The M1A1 has two large stowage boxes on either side of the turret. Hung on the side of the turret are identification panels to distinguish friendly vehicles while using thermal sights. The open ammunition box in the center of the picture is attached to the loader's M240 mount.

Below: The turret side stowage box lids are held secure by two locking handles. In common with virtually all tanks since their inception, the interior of the vehicle lacked sufficient space for stowage, therefore requiring these external compartments. The turret boxes are used to primarily to store tank maintenance equipment and some crew gear (helmets). Crew bags go into the bustle rack/bustle rack extension.

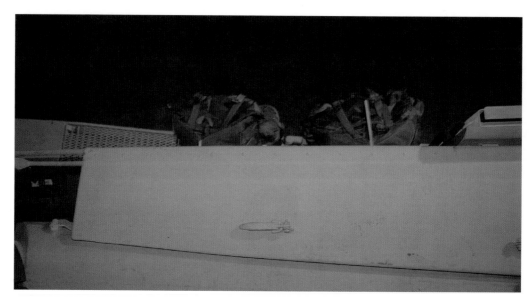

The MIAI is equipped with a large rear turret stowage basket. Here the rack is filled with small-arms ammunition boxes and a 5-gallon liquid container. A spare road wheel is attached to the bin by a bolt and a track center guide horn.

The sheer size of the Abrams, combined with its smooth surfaces (compared to previous tank designs) made boarding the vehicle challenging. Thus the design included these short lengths of cable on the bottom of the armored skirts, forming crew steps.

The Abrams is fitted with seven paired road wheels per side. The wheels mount a 25 x 5.69in solid rubber tire. The road wheels are suspended by a high-strength steel torsion bar allowing 15in of wheel travel.

The forward fuel tanks are filled through points in each side of the front glacis plate. The fuel capacity of the tank is 505 US gallons, giving a cruising range of approximately 290 miles.

Above: This area of the glacis is covered by the overhang of the forward portion of the turret. The clip to the right the filler is a stop for the open driver's hatch.

Below: The armored skirts are hinged in various directions to allow access to the suspension to perform maintenance. The black chevron markings were present on all Coalition forces in Operation Iraqi Freedom.

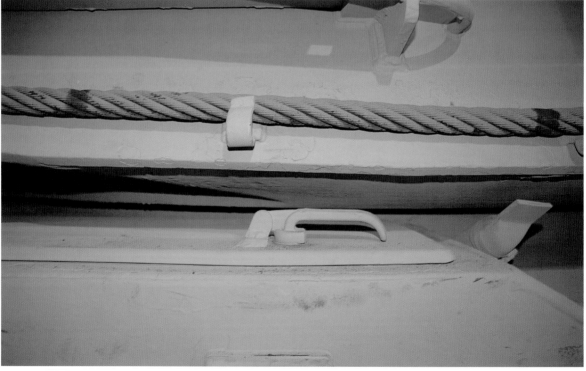

Above: The rear handles on the hull side storage compartments have a locking flange which is secured here by a bolt. In service, the hull stowage boxes contained larger maintenance tools such as the tankers bar, shovel, axe and sledge hammer.

Opposite above: Above, the right side turret overhang is the outlet for the hull bilge pump. Above the tank's tow cable is stored in clips on the turret side below the stowage bin.

Opposite below: Each side of the hull is equipped with a shallow stowage bin. The hinged lids are secured by locking handles. Note the weld seams on the brackets for the turret side stowage bins.

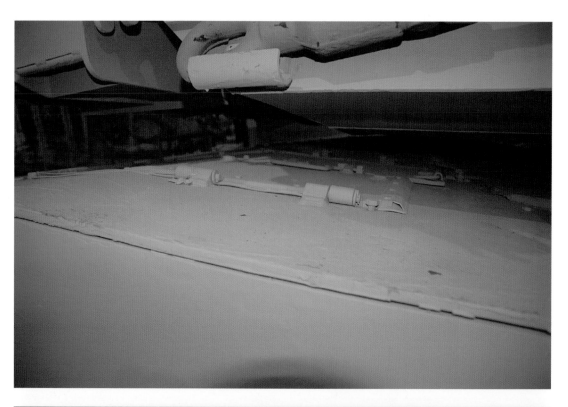

Above: This display tank is fitted with many common items of gear seen on tanks during OIF. The ammunition boxes are for 5.56mm (.223 cal.) weapons; there are the ubiquitous plastic 5 gallon liquid containers. A foam pad for a sleeping bag is wrapped and secured around the antenna mount.

Opposite above: The air intake openings are protected by screens. They are sealed tight against the deck to keep any debris from entering around their edges. The rear clip for the tow cable is seen at the top of the picture.

Opposite below: The stowage bins on the M1A1 turret sides are much large than the earlier models, extending well toward the turret rear. The packs in woodland camouflage contrasts greatly with the sand paint of the Abrams.

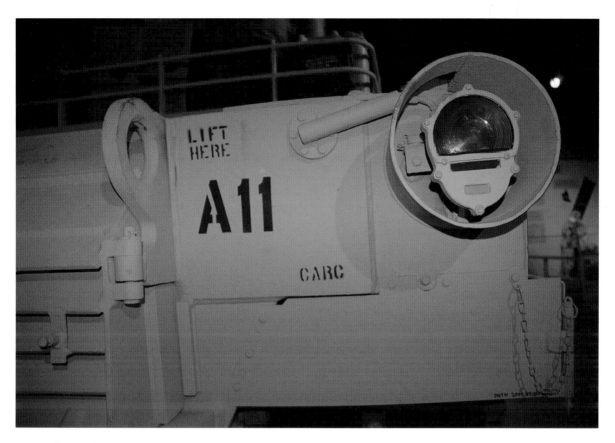

Above: The right rear tail light is protected by a steel bezel. The tail light has a blackout lens below the red plastic lens. Note the tubular protection for the light's power cord.

Opposite above: The right sprocket is viewed close-up. Four D-shaped lightening holes are arranged in the sprocket drum. Sixteen lug nuts are around the inner perimeter of the drum, and there is a cross-shaped hubcap, secured with four hex screws.

Opposite below: The display tank is equipped with the T158 "Bigfoot Track" with the octagonal rubber contact shoe. The track is 25 inches wide with a pitch of 7.625 inches. It is a dual pin live track with replaceable pads.

Above: The right side rear grill is hinged to allow access to the right side transmission oil cooler This display tank is missing the steel grilles that deflect the engine exhaust and engine & transmission oil cooler exhaust air directly behind the tank.

Below: The center grill on the rear hull is for the engine exhaust and is often seen with the paint cooked off and the metal discolored. The black finish here is applied paint.

The left side grill is also for airflow through the transmission oil cooler. It is hinged at its left side for access. Just above the hinges is the rear hull lift ring.

The left side tail light also has a protective metal bezel. The blackout apertures at the base of the lights are used to maintain a safe driving distance when following another vehicle without the use of headlights.

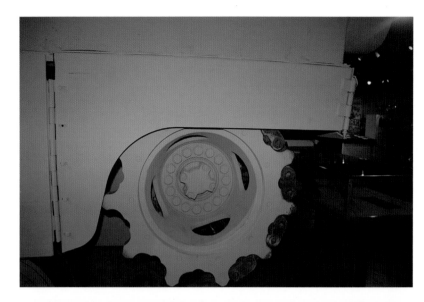

The rear skirt on the Abrams series was modified to help alleviate the track throwing problems of the early models. This helped to prevent a build up of mud in the area of the drive sprocket. A mud scraper was also added to the hull side.

The central portion of the engine deck is secured by bolts but can be removed in minutes. With this large plate out of the way and the rear grills swung aside the access to the engine compartment is tremendous.

The right rear corner of the engine deck mounts the filler for the rear fuel tank. In both campaigns in Iraq, the speed of advance of the M1A1 created a great challenge to keep fuel and spare parts available.

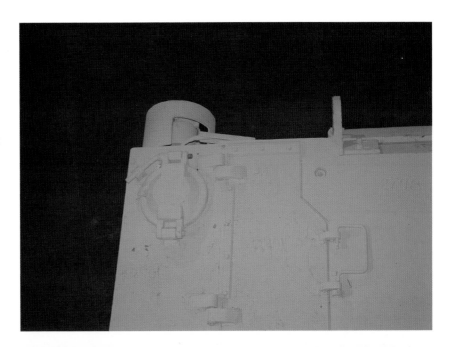

The left rear corner of the hull houses a large fuel tank filled at this point. Most of the upper surfaces of the tank are covered with a rough anti-skid coating.

The left side fuel tank cover overlaps the rear of the hull side. The hinge system for the armored side skirts is visible at the joints between the panels.

The hull side armor, although still formidable, is thinner in the area around the engine compartment to save weight. The tank's design emphasized crew survivability.

The details of the left side turret are from the left, the stowage box, turret side basket, tow cable stowage clips, and turret bustle rack. It is doubtful that a crew would have stowed the ammunition boxes in this area without securing them.

The left side turret stowage bin has two woodland camouflage ALICE packs attached. In both Gulf conflicts gear with coloring more suitable for a European battlefield is often seen on vehicles.

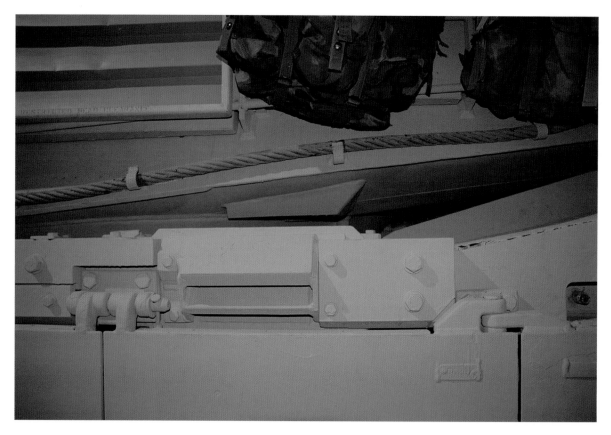

One upgrade incorporated in MIAI production was the NBC filtration system, the inlet being just forward of the fire suppression system handles on the left hull side. The NBC system is an overpressure and climate control device to protect the crew from nuclear, biological, or chemical attack.

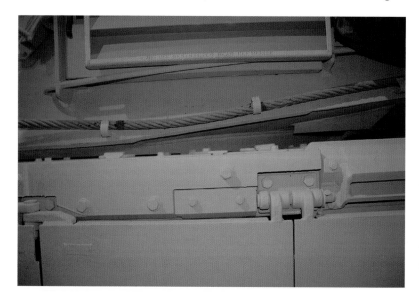

The complex hinge system on the armored side skirts allow the crew to service various portions of the suspension by folding different portions of the skirt in different directions. The bolted plate above the skirt is a cover for the NBC system.

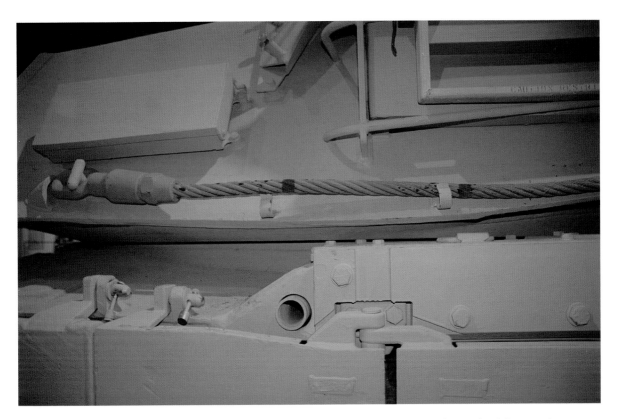

Just forward of the NBC system is an exhaust for the crew heater. Note the method for securing the forward cable end on the turret side.

The left turret side mounts a rectangular storage box for smoke grenade rounds. The rounds are loaded into the muzzle of the M250 launcher, making the storage of the rounds near the device very convenient. There is a small bullet splash welded to the turret side forward of the cable bracket.

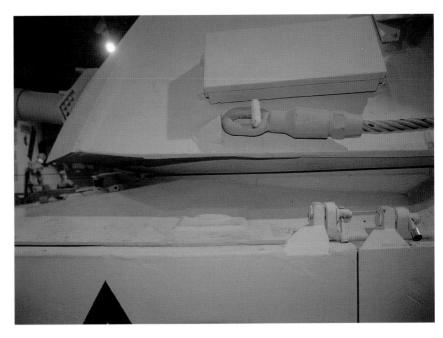

Chapter 5

Mine Plows and Blades

Above: A fact of modern warfare is that small, cheap, explosive devices can still defeat a multi-million-dollar, state-of-the-art tank. To counter this threat, in the 1980s the military began implementing in Abrams tank units an inexpensive response: the mine plow. The idea was to unearth and push to the side any buried mines in the path of a column. Shown here is an MIAI with a mine plow in the retracted position passing a destroyed enemy SUV during Operation IRAQI FREEDOM. (*Department of Defense*, hereafter *DoD*)

Opposite above: The MIAI is capable of carrying the Full-Width Mine Plow (FWMP) built by Pearson Engineering. The device is attached to the internal hydraulics of the vehicle for operation. (*Don Moriarty*)

Opposite below: The center section of the unit can be removed to convert the unit to clear a lane width. The device can clear a width of 13ft 10in in full-width mode. (*Don Moriarty*)

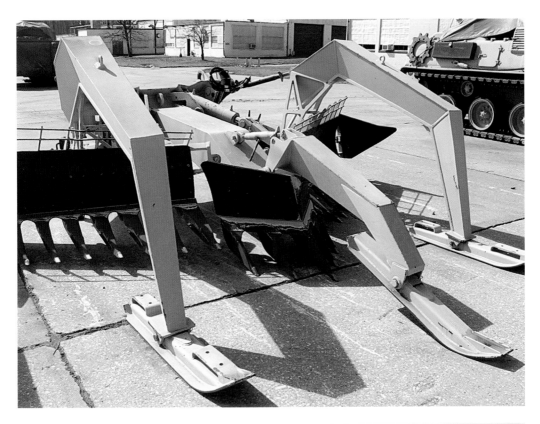

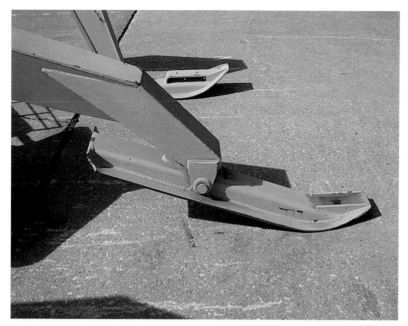

Three ski-like projections are mounted on the front of the unit. These help to carry some of the weight of the plow while operating. The unit weighs approximately 4 tons. (*Don Moriarty*)

The attitude and angle of the plows can be adjusted hydraulically to set the depth at which the plows run. The plow must be raised in order to turn the tank or the plows may break in the ground. (*Don Moriarty*)

The plow is designed to lift a mine from the ground without exploding it and then sweep it to the side down the 'V'-shaped blade. If the mines are exploded, this will be done at a safe distance from the operating vehicle. (*Don Moriarty*)

The plow clears a lane when attached to a lead vehicle, allowing other vehicles to follow in safety. The use of the plow reduces the speed of an Abrams to below 10 mph. (*Don Moriarty*)

The mounting points for the plow are common to the dozer blade attachment and the surface-clearing device (SCD). The FWMP can be fitted with a magnetic signature duplicator to protect it from magnetic mines. (*Don Moriarty*)

The FWMP is also fitted to the Assault Breaching Vehicle, an engineer vehicle based on the Abrams chassis. The plows are not popular with Abrams crews due to the reduction in speed of operation. (*Don Moriarty*)

The rear of the unit mounts hydraulic cylinders and hoses to feed power from the vehicle's hydraulic system. The two feet make the unit easier to attach to a vehicle from its storage position. (*Don Moriarty*)

The hydraulic cylinders can be used to lift the plows from the ground with the forward supports still supporting the weight of the unit. The main hydraulic lines are seen lying over the left side of the unit. (*Don Moriarty*)

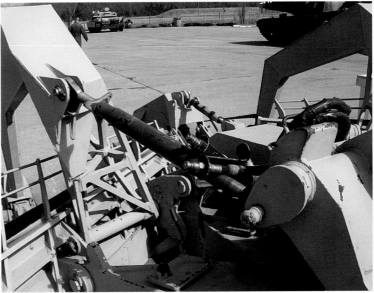

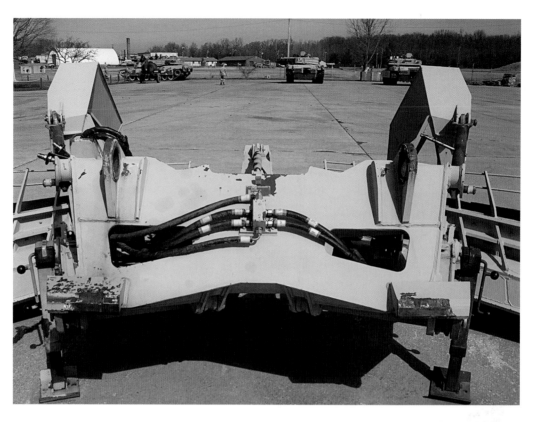

Above: The M1 series can also be fitted with a dozer blade attachment. The UDK-1 Heavy Dozer Blade is manufactured by Pearson Engineering. The width of the blade is 12ft 1in with a hardened steel cutting edge. This type blade is used by the USMC on their tanks, while the Army uses either the FWMP or dozer. (*Don Moriarty*)

Opposite above: The rear of the unit attaches to the glacis with the large upper rings. The lower bumpers rest against the front lower plate to support the weight of the unit. The mounting bracket is a massive welded assembly. (*Don Moriarty*)

Opposite below: An M1A1 Abrams tank is equipped with a Pearson UDK-1 dozer, seen here in the raised position. On the underside of the blade is a heavy-duty network of reinforcing gussets. Visible above the rear of the turret are two tube-shaped CREW (Counter-Radio-Controlled Improvised Explosive Device Electronic Warfare) devices. (*USMC*)

The UDK-1 is designed to withstand the forces that the Abrams is capable of exerting on it during operation. It can be mounted to any Abrams or engineer vehicle. The unit weighs 4,960lb. (*Don Moriarty*)

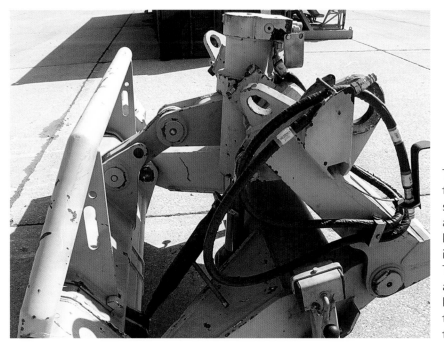

The UDK-1 attaches to the hydraulic system of the vehicle and can raise and lower the blade by internal controls. The blade is compact and its overall length keeps its mass close to the front of the tank. (*Don Moriarty*)

The unit can be lowered to scrape to a depth of 7in. It gives the Abrams an earth-moving capability for various tasks such as filling anti-tank obstacles or preparing defensive positions. (*Don Moriarty*)

Like the Full-Width Mine Plow, the upper attachment is made on the upper glacis and the bottom rests against the front lower armor plate. The feet on the unit store the device at a height for easy installation. (*Don Moriarty*)

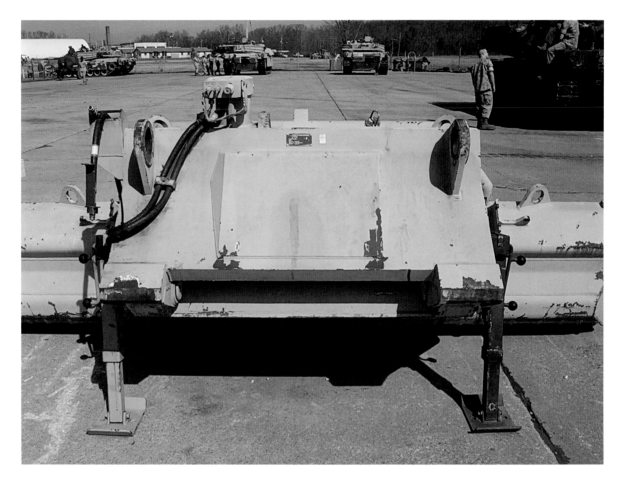

Above: The massive construction of the blade and mounting bracket are evident from this rear view. The paint has worn to bare metal from the dozer unit at all mounting and contact points. (*Don Moriarty*)

Opposite above: The back side of the blade is made up of various plates welded together to provide extreme strength while keeping weight to a minimum. The contours of the assembly are visible in the low rear view. (*Don Moriarty*)

Opposite below: This straight-blade surface-clearing device can also be mounted to the Abrams. Known as the Rapid Ordnance Removal System (RORS), it is manufactured by Pearson Engineering. (*Don Moriarty*)

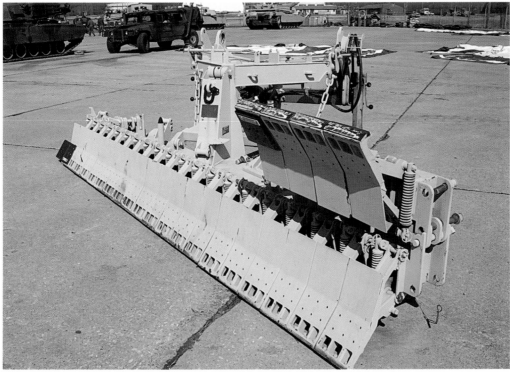

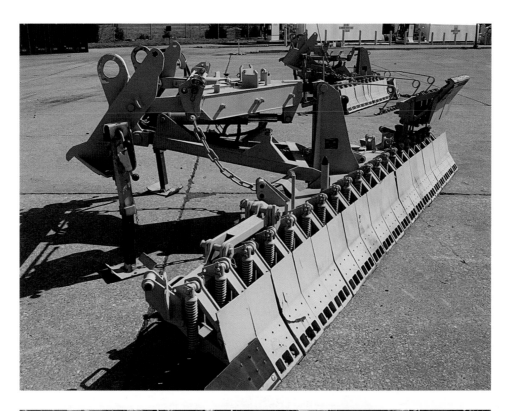

Above: The SMCD has a recommended operating speed of up to 10 mph. It is a heavier device than the RORS at 3,164lb and can clear a lane 14ft 10in in width. (*Don Moriarty*)

Opposite above: The straight blade weighs 2,866lb and attaches to the host vehicle's hydraulic system. It allows the vehicle to clear surface-laid mines and munitions for fast area clearance. It is 13ft 9in wide. (*Don Moriarty*)

Opposite below: The device is also manufactured in a 'V'-shaped configuration known as the Surface Mine-Clearing Device (SMCD) or Surface Mine Plow. The 'V'-shaped device is the preferred tool for route clearance of prepared roads. (*Don Moriarty*)

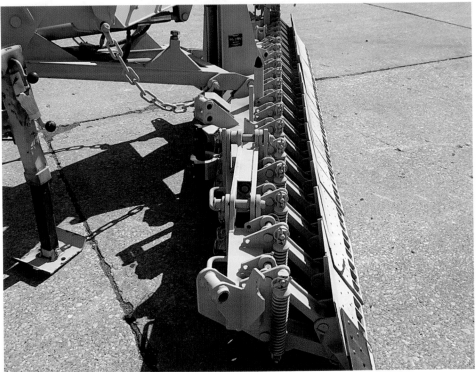

Above: The unit is designed to be as robust as possible at a minimum weight. This helps to keep the effects on the tank's performance to a minimum. (*Don Moriarty*)

Opposite above: The SMCD is designed to sweep any surface munitions to the side of the lane without exploding them. If they are detonated, the device is designed to absorb the energy at a safe distance from the vehicle. (*Don Moriarty*)

Opposite below: The blade of the RORS is made up of numerous short sections with a spring-loaded mounting allowing the blade to adjust to the contours or crown of the operating surface. (*Don Moriarty*)

The SMCD can also be fitted with a device that carries a length of heavy chain ahead of the blade in an attempt to detonate any munitions even further from the vehicle. (*Don Moriarty*)

The spring-loaded mounting arms allow the device to adapt to the contours of the surface being cleared. The blade sections on the heavier SMCD are taller than on the RORS. (*Don Moriarty*)

The chain device on the SMCD extends approximately 2ft from the blade for an added degree of safety from any IEDs. The device can be fitted to any Abrams or MI series-based engineer vehicle. (*Don Moriarty*)

The outside of the blade is equipped with a lane-width marker pole. This helps the driver to better judge the edge of the blade from the limited view in the driver's position. This device is operated with the driver's hatch closed for safety. (*Don Moriarty*)

Chapter 6

M1A2 SEP

Above: The latest upgrade to the Abrams family is the M1A2 SEP, or Systems Enhanced Package. The main external identifying feature of the M1A2 series is the commander's independent thermal viewer on the left turret roof.

Opposite above: The M1A2 has a heavier design to the rear engine exhaust grille, improving protection from the rear. The majority of the M1A2 series are actually converted from older M1 tanks during a rebuild.

By March 1992 an updated version of the Abrams had reached the prototype stage. The main internal difference to the vehicle is the integration of digital electronic controls to the tank. The new tank was named M1A2; the key external difference is the round aperture housing the commander's independent thermal viewer (CITV) in the left-side roof of the turret. This sight gives the commander the ability to acquire a second target while the gunner is engaging the first. This device was eliminated from the original design as a cost-saving measure.

The initial production contract with GDLS was for sixty-two new tanks. The US M1 fleet was aging, and a decision was made to convert many of the old 105mm-armed M1 to M1A2 standards.

The M1A2 in this volume is an M1A2 SEP (Systems Enhanced Package), which first entered service in 2001. The tank is equipped with the most modern digital hardware with improved microprocessors and memory. This has greatly improved the accuracy of the fire-control system. The tank also has improvements to the armor array of the turret and hull sides, and a new climate control system to cool the crew.

The left rear of the hull mounts the taillight in a protective circular guard. A small identifying plate is welded to the hull rear to the right of the taillight.

During the conversion to M1A2 standard the tanks receive a new set of engine exhaust grilles. The heavier construction is part of the improved armor package of the M1A2 design.

The infantry phone box is maintained on the right rear corner. The size of the slave receptacle for jump-starting the vehicle has been reduced. The M1A2 SEP has a new 'Silent Watch' battery system.

Even with the weight increase to 68 tons, the M1A2 mounts the same T158 25in-wide track. The large contact area of the tank's track provides excellent floatation for a vehicle of this weight.

The rear section of the side skirt has a hinge at its back edge. The hinge is equipped with a quick-release pin with a securing chain to prevent its loss. This allows quick opening of the side panel for servicing.

The belly armor of the Abrams is quite smooth with few obstructions. Unlike earlier US tank designs, the Abrams has no bottom escape hatch. Such a hatch would compromise the strength of the floor plate. The floor armor is contoured at the edges to accommodate the anchors and mounts for the torsion bars. The Abrams' central ground clearance is 19in. impressive for a vehicle with such a low silhouette.

Above: Centered in the lower hull rear armor plate is a mount for a tow pintle. Above the pintle is the lower edge of the grille doors which are considerably thicker than those of the M1A1.

Below: At the outer edge of the rear hull plate are tow lugs. These are often seen carrying the quick-release tow clevises for attaching a cable. The horseshoe-shaped clevises were a common sight in Operation IRAQI FREEDOM.

Above: The new arrangement of the heavier exhaust grilles is an identifying feature of the M1A2 series when seen from the rear. Survivability was one of the main goals of the M1A2 program.

Below: The right rear corner of the engine deck mounts the filler for the right-side rear fuel tank. The cover for the battery box is hinged and just inboard of the fuel tank cover.

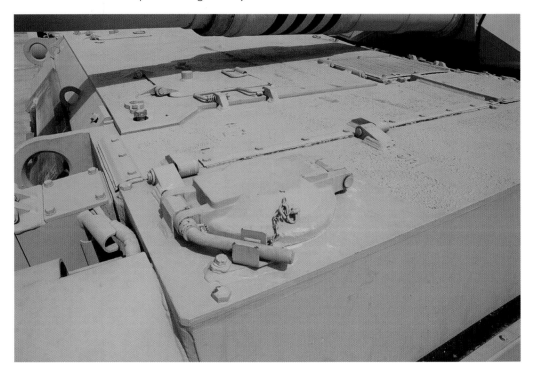

Above: From overhead the air intake screens are just inboard of the battery box doors within the rear deck. The small hinged doors at the rear of the deck are for quick access to the transmission oil coolers. Powder stains are present on the coaxial machine gun flash suppressor.

Below: At the extreme left rear of the rear deck are three hinged covers for the Under-Armor Auxiliary Power Unit (UAAPU). The screens visible at the lower right of this photo, forward of the UAAPU, cover the engine main air intake. The UAAPU occupied space previously filled by a fuel cell. The UAAPU failed to live up to expectations, and were eventually replaced by a second battery box. The screens in the center of the photo cover the air intake for the oil cooler.

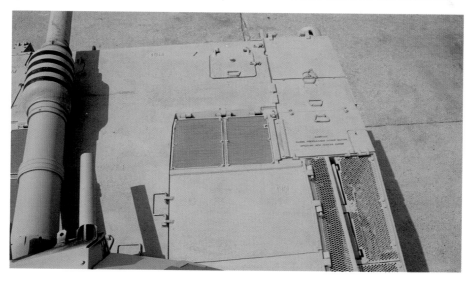

Above: The MIA2 is very similar in profile to the earlier MIA1, the height of the circular commander's independent thermal viewer being the only external visual difference from this angle. The bustle rack extension is quite long.

Below: The drive sprocket on this MIA2 is of a new design with the scallop on the inside of the sprocket ring. By comparing this to the view on page 74, one can clearly see the progression of the drive sprocket design.

The M1A2 retains the customary 25in road wheels of the Abrams family. The center hubs are fitted with a clear plastic cover that serves as a sight gauge of bearing lubricant within.

The right-side track ahead of the first road wheel runs up to the compensating idler wheel. The idler is linked to the first road wheel to adjust track tension based on movement of the road wheel over rough ground.

The M1A2 SEP is fitted with combat identification panels on the side and rear of the turret. These panels provide a distinctive shape through a thermal sight to identify the vehicle as friendly.

The rear combat identification panel is marked with the vehicle's number. The vapor compression system unit (VCSU) is visible in the bustle to the left of the panel. The VCSU is a climate control system.

Power supply and piping for the new VCSU is run under the bustle rack beneath an armored cover. The VCSU can maintain interior temperatures below 95 degrees, even when the exterior temperature exceeds 120.

Below the left side of the bustle rack, one section of the cover for the VCSU cabling is equipped with quick-removal clips for fast access to service or disconnect the unit. This is positioned just below the unit.

Above: The M1A2 SEP is equipped with three antennas on the turret bustle roof. This is a part of the digital single-channel ground and airborne radio system (SINCGARS) first installed on the M1A2 SEP. The thin antennas are for the SINCGARs radios while the thick antenna is for the Enhanced Position Location Reporting System (EPLRS) which provides connectivity for the Force XXI Battle Command Brigade and Below (FBCB2) battlefield awareness (command & control) system. FBCB2 used the EPLRS to communicate with other systems, while the Blue Force Tracker is virtually the same system but uses satellites to communicate back and forth. Both depict the friendly and enemy positions on a digital map as well as having a reporting and messaging (chat) capability.

Opposite above: The smoke grenade storage box on the M1A2 SEP has a different hinge arrangement to older models. This is apparent when comparing this view with the one on page 104.

Opposite below: The inlet and covers for the NBC system are on the left-side edge of the hull. These parts are heavier in construction than those on earlier Abrams variants.

Above: The left-side rear road wheel station equipped with the clear plastic hub cover. These covers speed the process of checking the lubricant rather than requiring a messy removal of the cover.

Below: The rectangular panels on the turret face are used along with the combat identification panels to quickly identify the tank. The dark corner markings are quickly recognizable through thermal sights.

The threaded fittings atop the gun shield are for the power conduits for the .50-caliber Counter-Sniper Anti-Materiel Mount (CSAMM), which uses a mount similar to the Telfare Device and mounts to the mantlet, above the main gun. The CSAMM was fielded as part of the Tank Urban Survivability Kit (TUSK) I package, used on both M1A1s and M1A2 SEPs in Iraq.

The commander's independent thermal viewer, here rotated to a protected position, allows the commander to track and acquire a second target while the gunner engages a first. This speeds the ability to engage multiple targets.

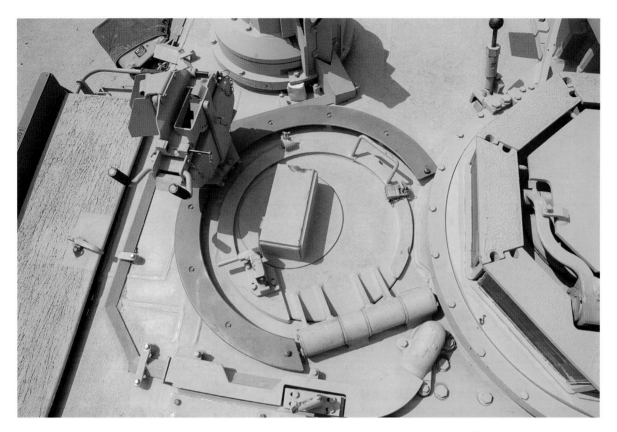

Above: The skate rail is left unpainted so as not to restrict movement of the M240 mount. The fitting to the left of the loader's periscope is a latch to secure the hatch in its open position.

Opposite above: The loader is provided with an M240 7.62mm light machine gun to provide additional firepower against infantry and lightly-armored targets. The gun is mounted on a skate rail around his hatch.

Opposite below: The mount for the M240 includes a locking mechanism to hold its position on the skate rail. Its black locking handle is seen at the base of the mount, well below the two black hand grips of the machine-gun cradle.

Above: The black disk on the CITV mount is the tank's GPS antenna that provides positioning data to the FBCB2 system. The same antenna is found on the back of the turret, in front of the crosswind sensor on M1A1 tanks.

Opposite above: The armored cover for the gunner's primary sight is forward of the commander's cupola. The gunner and commander are provided with a position/navigation system on the M1A2 SEP to provide vehicle location without a satellite link.

Opposite below: The M1A2 is equipped with an improved commander's weapon station mounting a .50 caliber or M240 machine gun. The weapon can only be fired with the hatch in the fully open position. On the M1A2 SEP V2, the ICWS has the machine-gun mount removed and a CROWS II remote weapon station is added on top of the gunner's primary sight housing.

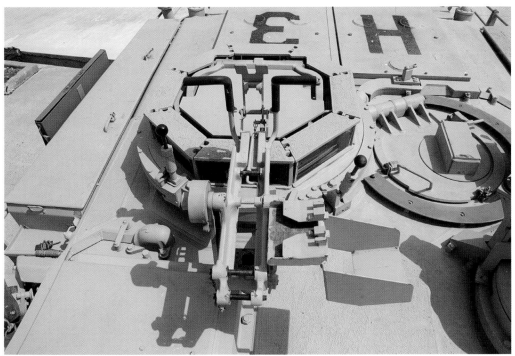

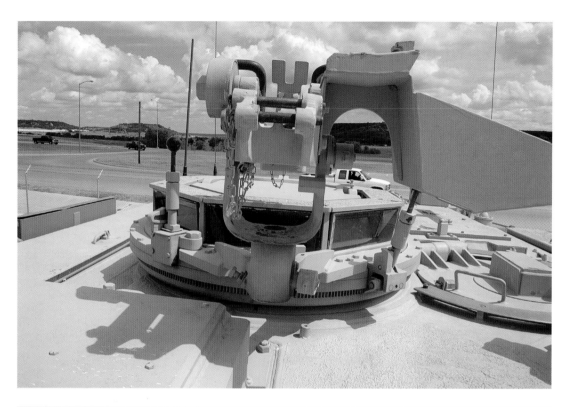

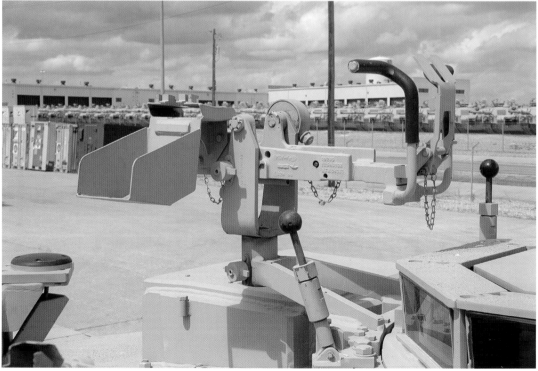

Above: All the commander's periscopes are laser-shielded to protect him from possible vision damage from battlefield lasers. The periscopes provide an overlapping view of 360 degrees.

Opposite above: The machine-gun mount rotates around the base of the commander's fixed cupola, which is fitted with six periscopes for 360-degree visibility. The earlier variants were equipped with a rotating cupola.

Opposite below: Here the machine-gun mount is viewed from the left side. The left side of the mount has a fixture for an ammunition box. The black circular device to the left is the GPS antenna for the CITV.

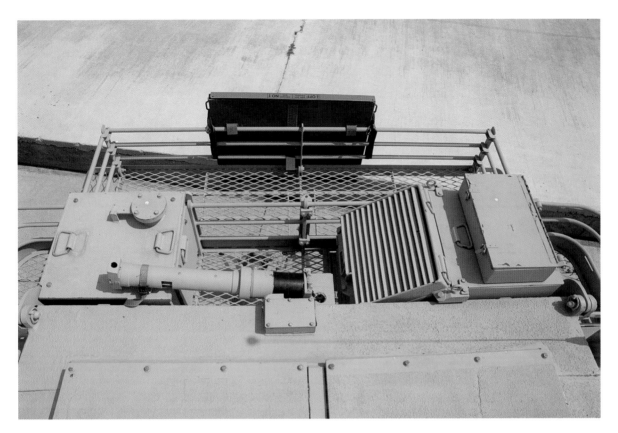

Above: The VSCU is on the right side and the armored box is for the CREW counter-IED jammer (most people know the CREW device as the DUKE). The thick tan FRC-105D antenna will mount on the round fitting on top of the box. The vapor compression system unit (VCSU) is mounted in the left rear portion of the turret bustle rack, which is to the right in this photo.

Opposite above: The commander's hatch cover is a heavily-armored assembly that provides a degree of protection for the lower back when in its open position. Anti-skid coating is visible on the periscope guard ring.

Opposite below: The turret blow-out panels above the ammunition storage have a different bolt pattern to earlier variants. The M1A2 carries an additional two rounds of ammunition in the turret racks.

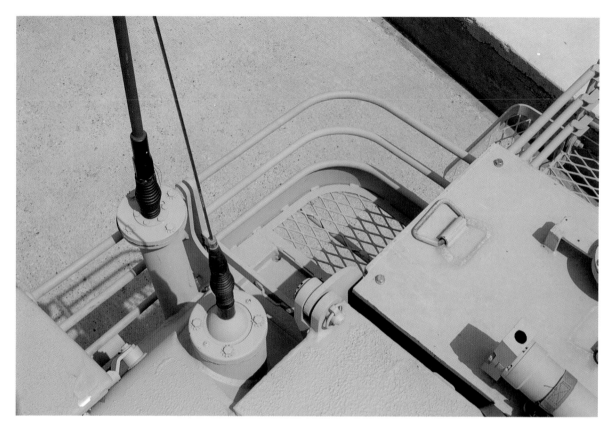

Above: To the right of the bustle rack are mounted two antennas for the single-channel ground and airborne radio system (SINCGARS). The radio system can transmit and receive digital, analog and voice signals.

Opposite above: Outboard of the VCSU in the bustle rack is room for additional stowage. Often this area is seen filled with two plastic 5-gallon liquid containers. The Abrams has ample area for stowing the crew's gear.

Opposite below: The layout of the turret has the commander behind the gunner on the right, with the loader on the left. The blow-out roof panels are visible behind the hatches.

Chapter 7

The Assault Breacher Vehicle

The US Marine Corps developed the Assault Breacher Vehicle (ABV) as a tracked armored-engineer vehicle tasked specifically with breaching minefields and complex obstacles. The Marine Corps started operating ABVs in February 2003. The key features of the ABV are a mine-clearing line-charge (MCLC) launcher to detonate mines, and provisions on the front of the hull for fitting a variety of attachments made by Pearson Engineering including a mine-clearing blade and a combat dozer blade. Here an ABV of the 1st Combat Engineer Battalion moves into position to fire an MCLC during Operation RAWHIDE in Afghanistan in March 2011. (*Official Marine Corps photo by Corporal John McCall*)

Shortly after the wondrous new weapon, the tank, crossed the battlefield in 1916, ambitious efforts began to create a system that would stop them. Among these efforts was the anti-tank mine. The initial efforts in this area consisted of merely burying a high-explosive shell upright so that the passing tank would activate the nose-mounted fuse of the round. Almost a century later essentially the same technique is being used, only now the weapons are called Improvised Explosive Devices. Of course, along the way there have been numerous specialized anti-tank mines developed, as well as myriad anti-personnel mines.

Through the years an impressive array of specialist vehicles has been deployed in efforts to forge a crossing of these minefields. These range from rollers to flails to plows and a host of other techniques. The recent conflicts in the Persian Gulf, with most of the combatants being an unseen enemy sowing a seemingly unending sea of IEDs, many capable of destroying the most formidable combat vehicles, pointed towards the need for a potent countermeasure.

The latest development in the US arsenal of such a system is the Marine Corps Assault Breacher Vehicle (ABV), based on the Abrams main battle tank chassis. Breacher vehicles have been included in Abrams planning for many years. The US Army had proposed, and indeed prototypes were built of, an Abrams-based breacher vehicle dubbed the Grizzly. The Grizzly program was cancelled in 2001 due to funding concerns. The Marine Corps, however, pressed on with the development of a breaching vehicle using its own funds. The result of this effort is the subject of this chapter, the Assault Breacher Vehicle (ABV).

In July 2003, the Marine Corps contracted with Anniston Army Depot to create three Production Representative Prototypes. Although utilizing refurbished Abrams hulls, the remainder of the vehicle is new, with a specialized turret and numerous systems mounted externally on the hull. Power is supplied by the same type AGT-1500 turbine that drives the Abrams, driving through a four-speed Allison X1100-3B Hydro-Kinetic automatic transmission. Engine and transmission are controlled by the driver from his position in the hull. The ABV's only other crewman is the weapons and communications system operator, stationed in the new custom-built turret.

Chief among the ABV's anti-mine systems are two M58 Mine-Clearing Line Charges (MICLIC). Each rocket-propelled line charge is 350 feet long and contains 5lb of C-4 per linear foot. Once detonated, each line charge clears a lane 8 meters wide. A lane-marking system is included in the vehicle in order to clearly delineate the safe path for following troops.

Also in the ABV's arsenal, and prominent in its appearance, is the specialized Full-Width Mine Plow (FWMP), developed by UK-based Pearson Engineering mounted on the front of the machine. The ABV is equipped for use with a variety of specialized Pearson front-end equipment beyond the FWMP. This includes the Rapid Ordnance Removal System (RORS) and a straight dozer blade known as the Combat Dozer Blade (CDB). The latter allows the ABV to prepare expedient firing positions and berms. All the various blades are equipped with Pearson High-Lift Adapters (HLA) that permit the rapid change of accessories while the crew remains under the protection of armor.

The first combat use of the ABV was during the assault on Now Zad, Afghanistan on the morning of 3 December 2009 as part of Operation COBRA'S ANGER. By that time Marine Combat Engineers had been training with the new vehicle for two years. The vehicles and their crews were an overwhelming success, with both performing fully as expected by Allied forces and completely surprising the Taliban with their capabilities. The vehicles cleared lanes with line charges and plows, detonating IEDs in the process. 'Breaching' is not confined to minefields, and ABVs deployed MICLIC into walled compounds, opening walls for infantry and decimating nearby defenders.

Once fully developed by the Marine Corps, and in light of the high rate of casualties among troops deployed to Iraq and Afghanistan, the ABV captivated the attention of the US Army, which was sufficiently impressed to order thirteen of the vehicles in 2010. Since then US Army orders have increased to 187 of the vehicles, while the Marines have ordered a more modest fifty-two of them.

Opposite above: The prototype of the ABV was photographed in 2006 and is shown without the Pearson or line-charge equipment installed. The ABV is not considered a version of the Abrams but is an autonomous system based on the Abrams chassis. (*Mike Mummey*)

Opposite below: The mounts for Pearson equipment on the front of the hull of the ABV prototype are in view. To each side of the deck to the front of the driver's hatch are headlights, raised to clear the attachments. Reactive armor tiles are mounted on the welded-steel turret. (*Mike Mummey*)

The ABV prototype is observed from its right rear. Up to the top of the hull, the ABV looks like any Abrams tank. Above the top of the hull, the construction is all new. The US Army Anniston Depot in Alabama designed and developed the ABV. (*Mike Mummey*)

Above the top of the hull of the ABV prototype, viewed from the right rear of the vehicle, is where equipment for the linear demolition charge (LDC) system, including storage bins containing the line charges, is located. To the right is a spare bogie wheel. (*Mike Mummey*)

The ABV prototype is maneuvering up to a full-width mine-clearing blade. Attachments can be made quickly to plows and other accessories, which also can be detached rapidly. To the front of the commander is a mount for a .50-caliber machine gun. (*Mike Mummey*)

The top of the turret is viewed from the right rear of the commander's cupola, showing the open hatch (left), periscope housings and .50-caliber machinegun mount of the cupola. Details of the design of the turret roof are also in view. (*Mike Mummey*)

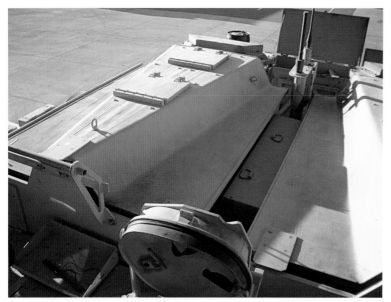

From atop the turret roof facing aft, the two covers of the linear demolition charge-launchers are in view. These have lifting eyes and access doors on their tops and are hinged at the rear and tilt upward when the line charges are to be fired. *(Mike Mummey)*

The ABV prototype is viewed from its left rear quarter. As on the Abrams main battle tank, the grilles at the rear of the hull are, from left to right, for the engine oil cooler, the primary transmission oil cooler, engine exhaust and auxiliary transmission oil cooler. *(Mike Mummey)*

Two production ABVs were photographed in February 2010 during exercises at the Marine Corps Air-Ground Combat Center, Twentynine Palms, California. The vehicle to the right, whose turret is traversed to the left, is fitted with a Pearson full-width mine-clearing blade with three skids for regulating the depth of the blade. An optional Magnetic Signature Duplicator (MSD) is designed to defeat magnetically-fused mines. (*DoD*)

The Pearson Engineering full-width mine-clearing plow is viewed from the front on a standard production ABV. The full-width plow can be converted to a track-width mine-clearing plow by detaching the center section. The photographs of this vehicle were taken in October 2009. (*Mike Mummey*)

Above: Hydraulic lines for the front-end attachments are routed under the cover on the deck to the left of the driver's hatch. These plows are powered by the vehicle's hydraulics using these lines. (*Mike Mummey*)

Opposite above: The center and left sections of the Pearson full-width mine plow are observed from the front right quarter. The design of the plow and its skids with their spidery legs is quite different from the design of the mine-clearance plows for Abrams MBTs. (*Mike Mummey*)

Opposite below: Details of the right fender and headlight and the reactive armor on the turret are in view. On the front deck of the hull below the turret is the driver's hatch with periscopes and fuel-filler covers. The side skirts are hinged for easy access to the suspension. (*Mike Mummey*)

Above: Forward of the lane-marker system units, the rears of the linear demolition charge-launchers are visible. Next to the left taillight on the rear of the hull is a radio antenna and mount. Stenciled on that mount is 'do not touch antenna while transmitting.' (*Mike Mummey*)

Opposite above: On the platform at the right rear corner of the turret is the right lane marker, folded in its stowed position. The lane-marking system (LMS) electro-pneumatically dispenses rods into the ground to mark mine-cleared routes. An LMS is also on the left side. (*Mike Mummey*)

Opposite below: In a rear view of an ABV, just forward of the three boxes at the rear of the turret are the left and right LMS units. They are loaded with markers; these are white with metal-colored points. Stenciled above the engine exhaust is 'exhaust generates extreme heat.' (*Mike Mummey*)

Above: The left LMS, folded down in the stowed position, is viewed from forward. Stenciled on the hull below it is the caution notice 'do not stand under LMS when deployed.' On the side of the turret is a spare bogie wheel with a short tow cable stowed around it. (*Mike Mummey*)

Opposite above: On each side of the turret is an eight-tube smoke-grenade discharger. Just aft of the discharger are two smoke-grenade stowage boxes. Two spare track links are below the boxes. The mount for the .50-caliber machine gun is also visible to the left. (*Mike Mummey*)

Opposite below: The Pearson full-width mine-clearing blade weighs 7,940lb. It can clear a lane approximately 14ft wide and to a depth of between 7in and 12in. The normal operating speed of the vehicle with the plow deployed is from 1 to 10 miles per hour. (*Mike Mummey*)

Above: An ABV of the Assault Breacher Vehicle Platoon, 1st Combat Engineer Battalion, USMC fires an MCLC to clear a path into the town of Bahram Chah, Afghanistan on 14 March 2011. Only the MCLC launcher cover of the ABV is visible to the lower right. (*Official Marine Corps photo by Corporal John McCall*)

Opposite above: During the mine-clearing operation at Bahram Chah on 14 March 2011, an MCLC has just detonated on the ground, destroying any mines and improvised explosive devices in the path. Each line charge fired by the ABV contains 1,750lb of C-4 explosive. (*Official Marine Corps photo by Corporal John McCall*)

Opposite below: After a US Marine ABV assigned to the Breacher Vehicle Platoon, 1st Combat Engineer Battalion, has cleared a lane at Bahram Chah, Afghanistan during Operation RAWHIDE on 14 March 2011, follow-on forces of the 3rd Light Armored Reconnaissance Battalion proceed along the now safe lane. On this occasion, improvised explosive devices (IEDs) were deemed to be a particular threat along this route, frequented by insurgents. (*Official Marine Corps photo by Corporal John McCall*)

Chapter 8

The Abrams Deployed

Above: The MI, like the XMI, was armed with a 105mm main gun. The MI could be differentiated from the XMI by the presence of the long, tubular flash suppressor for the 7.62mm coaxial machine gun positioned to the right front of the 105mm gun shield. (*TACOM LCMC History Office*)

Opposite above: During Operation DESERT STORM, a member of the 1st Cavalry Division 'First Team' lifts a 105mm armor-piercing, discarding-sabot (APDS) round. The black-colored sabot flies off when the projectile exits the barrel. Yellow caution stickers are visible on the projectiles. (*DoD*)

Opposite below: On a hazy or dusty day in Saudi Arabia during Operation DESERT SHIELD, a crewman stands on the glacis of an MIAI that is still painted in woodland camouflage. On a skirt panel is a tactical symbol: a circle with a diamond inside it, in which is the number 66. (*3ACR Museum*)

Above: Churning up thick dust and exhaust, an MIAI with 4th Platoon, G Troop, 3rd Armored Cavalry Regiment is speeding across the desert in Saudi Arabia. The vehicle has an overall sand camouflage scheme. Indistinct artwork is on the side of the turret directly above the platoon number 4. (*3ACR Museum*)

Below: Operations in DESERT SHIELD made it clear that the M88AI was not an adequate recovery vehicle for the Abrams, leaving tankers to use Abrams to retrieve Abrams as seen here. On the rear of the turret bustle and on the skirt of this MIAI are tactical symbols consisting of a circle with a pentagon within it, inside of which is the Roman numeral IV above the number 2. A dozen machine-gun ammunition boxes are strapped to the side of the turret. (*3ACR Museum*)

Above: A hoist is positioning a mine-clearing blade system onto the bow of an MIAI in Saudi Arabia. To the left of the crewman in the parka are two skids, which acted to limit the depth of the cut of the plow blades. The plows excavated buried mines and pushed them to the sides of the vehicle for disposal. (*3ACR Museum*)

Below: Dust storms occasionally brewed up to add to the discomforts of combat personnel during the Gulf War, as the crew of this MIAI could attest. Such storms diminished visibility and added to the maintenance duties of the crews in order to combat the damage the dust could do to various systems in the tank. (*3ACR Museum*)

Above: The M1A1 of the commander of G Troop, 3rd Armored Cavalry sits at the ready in the desert during the 1990–91 Gulf War. The sand-colored camouflage blended well with the terrain during this operation. (*3ACR Museum*)

Below: At an assembly area in the desert, crews of two M1A1s of Troop G, 3rd Armored Cavalry relax, including a man sleeping on the engine deck of the nearest tank. The large roll of concertina wire on the rear of that tank would be used for security precautions at bivouacs. In the background is a row of three Bradley fighting vehicles with orange recognition panels on the turrets. (*3ACR Museum*)

Above: Several M1A1s from the 4th Platoon, G Troop, 3rd Armored Cavalry Regiment have paused in the desert. The crewman on the ground in the foreground is using compressed air to blow the dust out of precleaners. According to reports, the Donaldson air precleaners used in M1A1s in the Gulf War were prone to frequent failure in the dusty environment. (*3ACR Museum*)

Below: A small guidon with markings for G Troop, 3rd Armored Regiment and a small US flag are flying from the antennas of an M1A1 during a pause in the 1990–91 Gulf War. Very faintly visible on the right front of the turret is artwork in black of a man on horseback, possibly an old-time cavalryman. (*3ACR Museum*)

Two Allied soldiers pose with a US crewman on the front of an MIAI assigned to G Troop, 3rd Armored Cavalry Regiment. Rations boxes are secured to the side of the turret and are stored on the turret roof. (*3ACR Museum*)

Wearing woodland patterned Chemical Protective Over Garments AKA CPOGs and one of them wielding a Bowie knife, members of an MIAI crew pose in front of their tank during the 1990–91 Gulf War. A spare bogie wheel is stored on the front left corner of the turret roof and the red object on the turret roof is a small boom box. (*3ACR Museum*)

In Operations DESERT SHIELD and DESERT STORM in 1990 and 1991, anti-tank mines were a serious and constant menace, the Iraqis having sown thousands of them in the region. To clear mines from lanes of advance, a mine plow designated the M1 Mine Clearing System was developed for use on the M1 and M1A1. The electrically-operated plow could clear mines on the surface or those buried up to 6ft deep. The plow also was useful in breaching berms and obliterating enemy entrenchments. (*3ACR Museum*)

During Operations DESERT SHIELD/ DESERT STORM, a group including Colonel Douglas H. Starr, commander of 3d Armored Cavalry Regiment, stands next to an M1A1 while visiting the 2nd Platoon of F Troop. Liquid containers and rations boxes are strapped to the side of the turret bustle. (*3ACR Museum*)

Above: Among the markings on the skirt of this M1A1 with the 3rd Platoon, H Troop, 2nd Squadron, 3rd Armored Cavalry Regiment during Operations DESERT SHIELD/DESERT STORM is a bit of tanker art: a depiction of a beach muscle-man wearing sunglasses. (*3ACR Museum*)

Opposite above: Crewmen from 2nd Platoon, Fox Troop, 2nd Squadron, 3rd Armored Cavalry Regiment pose next to an M1A1 during Operations DESERT SHIELD/DESERT STORM. Marked on the armored skirt is 'F2' ('F' standing for Fox Troop and '2' for 2nd Platoon) and a stencil of a fox's head, below which is lettered 'FOX'. Judging by the men's dress, the photo was taken in the latter part of 1990 or early 1991. (*3ACR Museum*)

Opposite below: Officers of H Company, 2nd Squadron, 3rd Armored Cavalry Regiment pose with an M1A1 with the nickname 'HIGHLANDER II' stenciled in black on the main gun barrel. On the top of the 120mm gun's muzzle is the muzzle reference sensor, part of a system for compensating the sighting system for bends in the gun barrel due to temperature and other forces. (*3ACR Museum*)

Above: Crewmen of the 2nd Squadron, 3rd Armored Cavalry Regiment commander's M1A1 tank pose on an abandoned Iraqi tank, either a Soviet-made T-72 or the Iraqi-built copy, called the Lion of Babylon. The inverted 'V' on the skirt of the Abrams was an Allied recognition sign during the 1990–91 Gulf War. (*3ACR Museum*)

Below: This 1st Tank Battalion, 1st Marine Division M1A1 uses its mine blade to push its way through an obstacle belt during a training exercise at Camp Pendleton in 1997. By then, the Abrams had been in service with the Corps for seven years, the transition from M60A1 tanks having begun in 1990. (*DoD*)

Beyond the mine-clearing blade, the Abrams can also use mine-clearing rollers, as demonstrated by this 3rd Armored Calvary Regiment M1A1 at Fort Polk, Louisiana. (*DoD*)

Sergeant Gary Owsley was photographed with two M1A1s of C Company, 1st Battalion, 635th Armor Regiment, Kansas Army National Guard at Yakima Firing Center, Washington in June 2002. Camouflage netting is wrapped around the 120mm guns. (*Gary Owsley*)

Above: The Grim Reaper, the 3rd Platoon logo, is visible on the smoke-grenade storage box near the front of the turret of this Abrams. The vehicle and crew are conducting live-fire training at Udari Range in Kuwait in December 2003. (*DoD*)

Below: 'Excellent Choice' leads a column of M1A1s of the 63rd Armor Regiment, 1st Infantry Division to support infantrymen in Kirkuk, Iraq in April 2003. The outside of the tanks are covered in gear, a situation that has existed as long as tanks have been on the battlefield. (*DoD*)

Above: During Operation IRAQI FREEDOM in 2003, Iraqi forces were ill-suited to contend with the US and Coalition forces invading the country. This knocked-out Iraqi T-72M1 is typical of the swath of destruction spread by the Abrams as the army advanced on Baghdad. (*3ACR Museum*)

Below: Abrams M1A2s of G Troop, 3rd Cavalry Regiment move past a roadblock during Operation IRAQI FREEDOM. The commander's independent thermal viewer is prominent on the turret roof of both tanks. (*DoD*)

Above: An IED has blown the turret off the hull of this MIAI; the rear of the turret is next to the rear of the tank and an external auxiliary power unit is visible on top of the turret bustle. The explosion also ripped the track from the tank, as well as much of the suspension. (*3ACR Museum*)

Opposite above: This MIAI, which has lost its left track and armored skirts, is being prepared for recovery. The turret has been swung to the right, placing the rear of the turret in the foreground. Visible is the external auxiliary power unit on the left and, rising next to it, the crosswind sensor that provides crosswind data into the fire-control electronics unit. Visible on the side and rear of the turret are the louver-like combat identification panels (CIPs) which help prevent friendly forces using thermal sights from targeting the tank. (*3ACR Museum*)

Opposite below: As the crew of another MIAI warily maintains vigil against insurgents, the crew of an M88 recovery vehicle has begun to extricate the disabled MIAI. The tank, which has lost its left tracking and whose right track is partially thrown, is settling deeply into the soft ground along the road, adding to the burden on the M88. (*3ACR Museum*)

Above: Enough is enough: during a firefight in Al Fallujah, Iraq on 10 December 2004, the crew of a 2nd Tank Battalion, USMC Abrams deals the final blow to a group of insurgents firing at Marines from the shelter of a building. Firing at point-blank range, the roar of the Abrams' 120mm gun levels the building, sending debris flying, pelting even the bright blue and white cooler on the turret roof with stones and grit. (*DoD*)

Opposite above: The turret blown off the M1A1 landed on the rear hull as well as the road. The panels atop the turret bustle blew off as designed, venting the force of any explosion of the 120mm ammunition upwards. In the foreground is an ammunition rack still attached to the blow-out panel. Visible on the loader's machine-gun mount, on the left top of the turret, is a Transparent Armor Gun Shield (TAGS). (*3ACR Museum*)

Opposite below: This Bravo Company, 2nd Battalion M1A1 has become deeply mired while operating near Sayyid 'Abd, Iraq during Operation IRAQI FREEDOM. Though often thought of as desert, there are many areas of soft, wet ground in Iraq that present a hazard for tanks in the location. (*DoD*)

Above: A pair of US Marine Corps M1A1 Abrams MBTs assigned to Bravo Company, 1st Battalion, 8th Marine Regiment, 1st Marine Division open fire with their main guns on suspected insurgent strongholds in Al Fallujah, Iraq. The Marines were taking part in a security and stabilization operation (SASO) carried out during Operation IRAQI FREEDOM. On the bore evacuator of the nearer tank is stenciled the moniker 'Maximus', while that on the other tank, which has a replacement forest green gun barrel, is 'Lion-Heart'. *(DoD)*

Opposite above: The crew of a 2nd Platoon, Bandit Troop, 1st Squadron, 3rd Armored Cavalry Regiment M1A2 prepares for a mission at Forward Operating Base Heider in Rabiah, Iraq on 27 June 2005. *(DoD)*

Opposite below: Several M1A1s of the Task Force 2nd Battalion, 34th Armor Regiment are returning to Camp Warhorse, Iraq on 5 December 2005. This force had just assisted Iraqi forces in the blocking and securing of Route Cheyenne leading into the city of Udaim. Although the company and order-in-column markings are visible on the Abrams in the background, the unit markings on the nearer tank apparently have been painted over, with only the number 3 visible. *(DoD)*

Above: With its turret traversed to the rear, an M1A2 with TUSK moves out from a base camp in Iraq. While rear-hull bar armor to protect that vulnerable area from projectiles was developed for the Abrams, it was never fielded. (*DoD*)

Opposite above: A Marine mechanic performs maintenance on a Regimental Combat Team 6 M1A1 at Camp Al Fallujah, Iraq on 21 January 2007. Two of the side-skirt panels are swung open, allowing the mechanic to inspect and service the suspension components. (*DoD*)

Opposite below: Several US Army M1A1s conduct an anti-IED operation on a highway in Baghdad on 22 December 2007. These tanks were equipped with a recently-updated Tank Urban Survivability Kit (TUSK) to better enable them to withstand attacks by insurgents. This includes a low armored shield on the turret roof around the loader's hatch. The yellow object sitting on top of the turret is a civilian-type water cooler. (*DoD*)

This M1A1 is undergoing an engine change. With the power pack removed, a mechanic easily stands in the interior of the white-painted engine compartment. At the front left of the compartment, two access hatches stand open, and at the rear the cooling and exhaust grilles have been swung open. This M1A1 is equipped with the TUSK and CREW enhancements. (*Russ Adams*)

Opposite above: At an equipment repair depot, two Abrams tank power packs have been removed from their vehicles. On the power pack to the left, the transmission is to the right and the Avco Lycoming AGT-1500 gas turbine engine is to the right. The power pack to the right is hitched to a sling attached to the hook of the crane boom above it. An Abrams power pack weighs approximately 8,500lb. In the background is the same M1A1 that appears in the preceding photo. (*Russ Adams*)

04.28.2010 16:99

The power pack is being pulled from a USMC Abrams tank at Camp Habbaniyah, Iraq on 29 June 2006. At the bottom rear of the unit is the Allison X1100-3B transmission; the dark-colored disk on the near side of the transmission is the output flange. Above the transmission are mounted, left to right, the engine oil cooler, the primary transmission oil cooler, the exhaust duct, and the auxiliary transmission oil cooler. (*USMC*)

Above: Marines from Alpha Company, 2nd Tank Battalion are about to refuel their MIAIs after a twenty-four-hour mission at Combat Outpost Shir Ghazay, Helmand Province, Afghanistan in August 2011. The first tank has a tow bar on the bow, the second tank has a mine-clearing blade system and both tanks have antennas for anti-IED systems on the turret bustles. (*DoD*)

Below: Members of Charlie Company, 1st Battalion, 8th Marine Regiment, Regimental Combat Team 6 confer with the crew of an MIAI from the 1st Tank Battalion, I Marine Expeditionary Force (Forward) during a patrol in Helmand Province, Afghanistan on 20 April 2012. (*DoD*)

Above: A US Marine Corps MIAI Abrams with anti-IED antennas on the turret bustle is about to be refueled at Combat Outpost Shir Ghazay, Afghanistan on 27 July 2012. The smoke-dischargers were a USMC type with eight individual launching tubes. To the front of the launchers is the storage box for the smoke grenades. (*DoD*)

Below: A USMC MIAI has completed refueling at Combat Outpost Shir Ghazay and is stirring up dust as it moves forward on 27 July 2012. Other MIAIs are to the left of this tank and in the background. On the rear of the hull is the base unit for attaching a deep-fording trunk. Sprocket retainer rings, which had been discontinued some time ago, were now reappearing on USMC Abrams tanks as a means of keeping the tracks in place, even when they were becoming slacker during extended operations. (*DoD*)

Above: US Marine Corps Brigadier General John J. Broadmeadow, in the camouflage boonie hat at center, commander of the 1st Marine Logistics Group (Forward), meets with his staff in front of a row of three M1A1 tanks during a pause in a combat patrol at Combat Outpost Shir Ghazay on 27 July 2012. The Abrams on the right is equipped with a Pearson dozer blade for clearing obstructions and leveling earth. (*DoD*)

Opposite above: Marine mechanics with Bravo Company, 2nd Tank Battalion use the boom of an M88A2 Hercules Armored Recovery Vehicle to reinstall the heavy armored decking onto an M1A1 Abrams tank, USMC registration number 632678, after an engine-change operation at Combat Outpost Shir Ghazay, Afghanistan on 4 November 2012. The scoop-shaped base for the deep-fording kit's exhaust trunk is visible on the opened exhaust grille. (*DoD*)

Opposite below: In a companion view to the preceding photo, the boom of an M88A2 Hercules is hoisting a power pack for the M1A1 to the right. The power pack was designed to allow for the rapid replacement, in the field, of the engine and the transmission. (*DoD*)

Above: A US Marine MIAI Abrams tank with mine-clearing roller installed from Delta Company, 1st Tank Battalion, Regimental Combat Team 7 makes tracks through an assembly area at Camp Shir Ghazay, Helmand Province, Afghanistan on 27 April 2013. Note the stretcher stored on the side of the turret and the roll of concertina wire stowed on the base of the left anti-IED antenna. Several folding cots are stored on the right side of the turret-bustle rack. (*DoD*)

Opposite above: Abrams tanks from Regimental Combat Team 7, 2nd Combat Engineer Battalion, 1st Tank Battalion and 3rd Battalion, 9th Marine Regiment are assembled during Operation DYNAMIC PARTNERSHIP in Shurakay, Helmand Province, Afghanistan on 11 February 2013. DYNAMIC PARTNERSHIP was a multi-unit effort to withdraw US military equipment and personnel from Shurakay district. The MIAI in the foreground is equipped with a mine-clearing roller (MCR), a heavy (20,000lb) assembly that detonates anti-tank mines. The rollers are designed to withstand multiple mine blasts before they require replacement. (*DoD*)

Opposite below: Two Marine crewmen of an MIAI are at their stations during Operation DYNAMIC PARTNERSHIP in Shurakay, Helmand Province, Afghanistan on 11 February 2013. The commander standing in the cupola is grasping a popular power drink. The other crewman has opened the cover of the receiver of his 7.62mm M240 machine gun and is using a brush to clean the receiver. A thermal sight is mounted on the receiver cover. (*DoD*)

Above: An M1A1 with Delta Company, 1st Tank Battalion, Regimental Combat Team 7 is parked at Camp Shir Ghazay, Afghanistan on 27 April 2013. A mine-clearing roller (MCR) is mounted on the front of the tank. The rollers detonated anti-tank mines only in line with the vehicle's tracks, so it was important for following vehicles to adhere closely to the track established by the tank with the MCR. (*DoD*)

Opposite above: The crew of a Marine M1A1 Abrams with Delta Company, 2nd Tank Battalion is maintaining surveillance over nearby compounds for potential threats during an operation in Helmand Province, Afghanistan on 8 August 2013. A stretcher is stored on the rear of the bustle rack, and camouflage net is rigged over the turret to protect the crew from the sun and snipers. Four two-link sections of spare track are mounted on the side of the turret. (*DoD*)

Opposite below: Marines of the 2nd Tank Battalion are preparing for a live-fire exercise with the new multi-purpose high-explosive rounds at a base at Shukvani, Afghanistan on 10 October 2013. The two nearest vehicles are M1A1s: the first one has the Pearson dozer kit, while the second has 'MULLIGAN!' stenciled in black on the bore extractor of the 120mm gun. The third vehicle is an M88 A2 Hercules Armored Recovery Vehicle. Towards the end of the line is an Abrams with a mine-clearing roller installed. (*DoD*)

Above: Personnel from the Marines' 1st Combat Engineers Battalion operating an M1 Assault Breacher Vehicle (AVB) nicknamed the 'Shredder' are detonating mines near Camp Leatherneck, Helmand Province, Afghanistan on 29 April 2014. The AVB has just fired an M58 Mine Clearing Line Charge (MICLIC), a rocket-propelled hose filled with Composition C (C-4) explosive, which has exploded, obliterating any mines and IEDs and clearing a path for troops and vehicles to pass through. (*DoD*)

Opposite above: The president of Estonia, Toomas Hendrik Ilves, right, rides in a US Army M1A2 with First Lieutenant Brian Van Vliet, a platoon leader with C Company, 2nd Infantry Battalion, 7th Infantry Regiment, 3rd Infantry Division at Jõhvi, Estonia, during Operation SIIL, a joint NATO exercise in May 2015. The Abrams has the Common Remotely Operated Weapon Station (CROWS) II RWS weapon station, an attempt to provide the TC the capability to engage targets while remaining under cover. The Transparent Armor Gun Shield (TAGS) and the loader's supplementary armor shields are part of the TUSK outfit. To the front of President Ilves is one of the defining features of the M1A2: the commander's independent thermal viewer (CITV), a sophisticated sighting device that allows the commander to acquire targets, communicate them to the gunner and then move on to the next target. (*DoD*)

Opposite below: An M1A1 Abrams and crewman from Delta Company, 1st Battalion, 4th Marine Regiment were photographed during a Coalition platoon attack drill during Exercise SsangYong 16 in South Korea on 17 March 2016. SsangYong is a biennial combined amphibious exercise conducted by forward deployed US forces with the Republic of Korea Navy and Marine Corps, Australian Army, and Royal New Zealand Army forces in order to strengthen the interoperability and working relationships of those forces. Note the large accumulation of .50-caliber spent casings and links on the front part of the roof of the turret and on the gunner's sight hood. (*DoD*)

Above: Rolling forward but with the turret traversed to the rear, a USMC M1A1 Abrams has just disembarked into shallow water from an Improved Navy Lighterage System Causeway Ferry during the Maritime Prepositioning Force offload phase of Saber Strike 17 on 24 May 2017. (*DoD*)

Opposite above: A column of M1A2 Abrams tanks from Company C, 2nd Battalion, 8th Cavalry, 2nd Infantry Division based at Fort Hood, Texas is crossing an engineer bridge over the Imjin River in South Korea during a joint US-South Korean combined-arms military exercise in April 2016. The tanks are equipped with MILES (multiple integrated laser engagement system), including gunfire simulators and various sensors. (*DoD*)

Opposite below: During a combined live-fire exercise during Exercise Saber Strike 17 at Adazi Training Grounds, Latvia on 9 June 2017, an M1A1 in sand camouflage from Alpha Company, 4th Tank Battalion, 4th Marine Division, Marine Forces Reserve moves downrange through a muddy draw. An annual combined-joint exercise conducted at various locations in the Baltic States and Poland, Exercise Saber Strike 17 trains NATO Allies and partners to meet regional crises and fulfill their own security requirements. (*DoD*)

Above: The crew of an MIA2 from the 1st Battalion, 9th Cavalry Regiment is awaiting its turn for a live-firing proficiency qualification in July 2017. The tank is outfitted with TUSK and has a combat identification panel (CIP), which looks like a louvered shutter, on the side of the turret. These panels, developed after Operation DESERT STORM, have a distinctive infrared signature when viewed through a thermal sight and help to reduce friendly-fire incidents. On the bow are the mounts for a mine-clearing roller. (*DoD*)

Opposite above: An MIA2 equipped with a mine-clearing blade is en route to gunnery qualifications at the Rodriguez Live-Fire Complex in the Republic of Korea on 4 August 2017. This tank was assigned to the Bravo Company, 1st Battalion, 9th Cavalry Regiment, 2nd Armored Brigade Combat Team, 1st Cavalry Division. The tan panels on the front facets of the turret are elements of the combat identification panel system. (*DoD*)

Opposite below: An MIA2 of Alpha Company, 1st Battalion, 8th Cavalry Regiment, 2nd Armored Brigade Combat Team, 1st Cavalry Division is moving to the next stage of its crew's gunnery qualifications at the Rodriguez Live-Fire Complex, Republic of Korea on 28 November 2017. During the next qualification, Table VI, the crew will be evaluated on its accuracy in engaging both stationary and moving targets in defensive and offensive postures. A good view is available of the prominent commander's remotely-controlled .50-caliber weapon station. (*DoD*)

Above: Thanks to the jumbo-sized air transports of today, it is possible to air-transport a heavy, sizeable tank such as the Abrams to distant hotspots with dispatch. Here, an M1A1 of the 1/118th Combined Arms Battalion ascends the ramp of a US Air Force Boeing C-17 Globemaster III at Wright Army Airfield, Georgia for transport to McEntire Joint National Guard Base, South Carolina. (*DoD*)

Opposite above: Another M1A1 Abrams is being offloaded from a Boeing C-17 Globemaster III under the supervision of members of the 386th Air Expeditionary Wing on 26 September 2013. Once in the cargo bay of the plane, the tank was firmly secured to the deck with a series of shackles. Although the cargo bay is very large, each C-17 can carry just one Abrams tank. (*DoD*)

Opposite below: A crewman of an M1A1 of the 2nd Tank Battalion, 2nd Marine Division, USMC registration number 584399, takes a break on the roof of the turret during a combined-arms exercise at the Marine Corps Air Ground Combat Center, Twentynine Palms, California on 1 February 2000. The nickname 'HIGHLANDER' is stenciled on the side of the bore evacuator of the 120mm main gun. (*DoD*)

Above: Abrams tanks proceed on a training exercise in the desert. The second tank is equipped with a Pearson UDK-I dozer. The barrel of the commander's .50-caliber machine gun of at least the lead tank is fitted with a blank-firing adapter (BFA), a fixture that must be fitted to that type of machine gun in order for it to fire blanks. (*DoD*)

Opposite above: A member of an Abrams unit performs maintenance on the suspension. This photo offers a rare view of the underside of the turret-bustle stowage rack to the left. On the bottom corner of the side of the turret is a casting number, 7511U, in raised figures. Stowed on the side of the turret over the spare track links is a collapsible-handle stretcher. (*DoD*)

Opposite below: In a view taken through a fish-eye lens, one of the tanks in a line of Abrams unleashes a 120mm round during a live-firing exercise. In the left foreground on the turret roof is the hood of a commander's independent thermal viewer (CITV), a feature of the MIA2 Abrams. To the front of this turret are a mount and an ammunition box for an external .50-caliber coaxial machine gun, a modification that gave the tank extra firepower for street-fighting and against unarmored vehicles. (*DoD*)

Above: Reactive-armor tiles are installed on the skirts of this TUSK-equipped M1A2, as well as ballistic shields for the commander's and the loader's machine-gun stations on the turret. On the main gun shield is the mount and ammunition box for the Counter Sniper/Anti-Material Mount (CSAMM), but these tend not to have been installed except when it was deemed that they were going to be necessary. (*DoD*)

Opposite above: Two crewmen check a .50-caliber machine gun on an M1A2. This model of the Abrams had a simple, manually-operated pintle mount for the commander's machine gun, which could be operated hands-on only, with the upper part of the body exposed outside the hatch. (*DoD*)

Opposite below: This photo presents an excellent view of the commander's and loader's ballistic shields on an M1A2 with the machine guns dismounted. The small stickers on the ballistic windows contain 'this side out' notices. Note the hinged rear panel on the loader's side armor. (*DoD*)

Above: Turret to the rear, an MIA2 kicks up dust as it moves through a gate in a security fence. The tank has the exterior coaxial machine-gun mount, reactive-armor tiles and ballistic shields for the commander and the loader. Two sections of steel fence posts, purpose unclear, are attached to the rear of the hull. (*DoD*)

Opposite above: The crews of two Abrams tanks of the 3rd Armored Cavalry Regiment conduct a combat patrol on the streets of Tal Afar, Iraq on 3 February 2005. Both tanks have the manually-operated commander's .50-caliber machine guns and the prominent CITV housings that are characteristic of the MIA2. The nearer tank has a ballistic shield for the loader's machine-gun station. (*DoD*)

Opposite below: The 120mm main gun emits an impressive blast as its USMC crew fires at a target during a training exercise in the western desert of Najaf Province, Iraq, on January 24, 2005. The vehicle and crew were assigned to Tank Platoon, Battalion Landing Team 1st Battalion, 4th Marines, 11th Marine Expeditionary Unit (Special Operations Capable). These tankers trained monthly in order to maintain their combat proficiency. (Department of Defense)

Appendix

Abrams specifications

Weight:	67.6 tons
Length, gun forward:	32.04 ft (IPM1) 32.25' (M1A1)
Hull length:	26.02 ft
Width:	12 ft
Height:	8 ft
Crew:	4 (commander, gunner, loader, driver)
Main armament:	105 mm L/52 M68 rifled cannon (M1) with 55 rounds
	120 mm L/44 M256 smoothbore cannon (M1A1, M1A2, M1A2SEP) with 42 rounds
Secondary armament:	1 x .50-caliber (12.7 mm) M2HB machine gun with 900 rounds
	2 x 7.62 mm M240 machine guns with 8,800 rounds
Engine:	AGT1500C multi-fuel turbine engine
Power/weight ratio:	24.5 hp/metric ton (18.27 kW/t)
Transmission:	Allison DDA X-1100-3B
Suspension:	Torsion bar
Ground clearance:	19 inches (M1, M1A1)
	18 inches (M1A2)
Fuel capacity:	500 gallons
Range:	300 miles
Speed, governed:	Road: 45 mph
	Off-road: 33 mph

AGT-1500 Specifications

Manufacturer- original, Lycoming; current, Honeywell

	English	Metric
Normal power	1,500 shaft horsepower	1,120 kilowatts
Torque @ 3,000 RPM	2,750 lb-ft	3,754 newton-meters
Total dry weight	2,500 pounds	1,134 kilograms
Fuel type	Diesel, jet fuel, gasoline	
Oil type	Synthetic	